Tachair and the Thum

Innis Macbea

Public entertainment is a harsh business. "More worship the rising than the setting sun," Pompey is reported to have said as Caesar moved to centre stage. Equally abrupt but less sanguinary has been the scrapping of *Tales of Tachair*, which filled our television screens for years, in favour of the ribald *Thumping Majority*, recording the ups and downs of an inner-city bank clerk who achieves rank and authority. Naturally there is a strong American influence: a whiff of *A Connecticut Yankee at King Arthur's Court* in the callous anachronism of the central character, and of *The Secret Life of Walter Mitty* in his inane dreams that come true.

Although *Thumping Majority* is represented as a spin-off from the Tachair series, and a few actors have appeared in both, the Major role has changed completely and the central joke is wholly different.

Chapman readers will recall that the name "Margaret Thatcher" is an anglicisation of the Gaelic *margadail tachair* ("marketable waterweed"), and so are those of all her associates and the weird, revolting and incredible creatures and practices among whom and which she dwells - with endearing exceptions like her consort "Denis" (*dionach* = "watertight"), loyally taciturn in an age of leaks.

The summary in *Chapman 40* had inevitably to be selective. It said nothing of the twin offspring of the pair, "Carol" and "Mark" (*ceardail* = "tinker-like", *marag* = "pudding"). The series includes several spots for Tink and Pud, but they are fairly humdrum on the whole although (as we shall see later) pudding provides a bridge between the series with the Rabelaisian touch we know so well. Before describing the transition to *Thumping Majority* it is useful to review some of the later Tachair canon, including the development of new twists amid the relentless flow of Gaelic puns.

Tachair and the Vile Morass

Although Tachair was born and raised in Grantham and a clerk she was of Oxenford also, (Geoffrey Chaucer (?1340-1400): *The Canterbury Tales*) most of the action of the series takes place in London. There is some difficulty about the syllable *Lon*, which varies in meaning depending on whether it is masculine or feminine or carries an accent. However, the favoured meanings in this context are either "morass" or "chatter" - and, given the authors' penchant for double meanings, why not both? *Don* signifies "evil" or "vile". There seems little doubt that Tachair's activities are in a vile morass in which evil chatter obscures reality and stretches credulity to the limit. A striking example of her approach is the episode of St James's Trash.

As a traditionalist, Tachair looks with concern on developments in London. For centuries the place has lived up to its name, exerting the fetid fascination on a certain turn of mind usually described as *nostalgie de la boue* (craving for the mud). A typical example is the twitching Scotophobe and anti-feminist Sam Johnson who, after surveying mankind from China to Peru, claims that in the Vile Morass there is all that life can afford (recorded in Boswell's *Life* as intoned on 20 September 1777); this bleak pessimism has blighted lives ever since. Great quantities of mud are lovingly scooped out of the sluggish rivers and streams that creep through the city, repeated epidemics and occasional great fires keep the populace in check and wild fish and animals disappear from the.polluted waters and rubbishy landward ground. But when Tachair emerges, strange and untoward things are happening in London. After centuries of justifying its name, the place is becoming increasingly clean and tidy and sensible talk is heard occasionally even among Tachair's own intimates.

With a bound she puts it right. (The perception that she is a bounder comes from Tam Dalyell, of the family of Dalyell of the Binns; his ancestral connection with bins perhaps explains why he and Tachair are mutually detestable.) Having reduced the country's capacity to earn by a quarter and committed great sums to building bases on the Howling Islands (see *The Smiting of Gealtaire* in Chapman 40), Tachair ordains that other public spending must be curtailed, particularly in the light of her need to reward the rich (who, she believes, work more productively if they are given more) at the expense of the poor (who are assumed to work harder only under threat of receiving less).

Since, by and large, it is the poor who earn a crust by clearing away the mess generated by the rich, this enlightened policy has the satisfying effect of restoring London to the vile condition in which Tachair and her creatures may prattle congenially. To complete the triumph, Tachair arranges for workers to sprinkle rubbish in the Park of St James, and in a much-loved episode ogles the cameras *while playing with it herself*.

Through the malign haze subordinate figures come and go, or even come back like *Paracas-sonn* ("rhapsodic stag", or Parkinson), who is forgiven his lapses and put in charge of destroying public transport and covering as much of the country as the defence budget allows with concrete. One by one, characters are written out of the script, like *Teabad* ("jeer", or Tebbit), whose sustained unpleasantness proves too much even for the mass audience, *Acair* ("thatch-stone", or Walker) and even, in a tizzy, the unpolluted wee hero himself, *Neoshalach Laochan* ("Nigel Lawson"). Across the western sea, there comes an even greater loss, which deserves a note to itself.

Tachair and the Moon Porpoise

Shortly after Tachair's elevation, the folk beyond the sunset find a new and perplexing leader. Although frequently depicted on an ordinary land horse with a name, "Reagan", that lends itself to the silly English pun "ray gun", this complex creature derives its name from *re* ("moon") and *cana* ("porpoise"). As one would expect, the loony and fishy nature of this character is set off by the playfulness and affability common to the dolphin family. There are even those who believe that dolphins are as intelligent as human beings, having large and crinkly brains, although they lack the vocal equipment to express themselves in human language. The Moon Porpoise is therefore amiable and incoherent, an ally after Tachair's heart. It even manages to have itself shot in the street so that she may hurry over to visit its sickbed, for one of her favourite practices is to visit the victims of mischance and disease, just as a reminder that things could be worse.

Tachair and Recana disport together for a whole eight years, confident in the knowledge that at least one of them is a *stupor mundi* and if not one the other (the script writers like to show their familiarity with foreign languages and, as we shall see, the crabbed wordplay of mediaeval schoolmen). And then, all of a sudden, the Moon Porpoise disappears and is replaced by a four-letter word normally associated with bad wine (a good wine needs no Bush). Thereafter, with the inevitability of a JICTAR rating, Tachair's sun moves towards its pathetic setting.

Maintaining the flow of characters in even a well-established soap puts great pressure on the creative writers as formulae grow thin; incident is less of a problem, so long as you can establish a character capable of anything. We see the writers even toying with hopelessly derivative material like this:

The Weird Sisters

Anglicised as Currie, Chalker and Rumbold, these three derive from *Cuaradh* ("torment"), *Siachaire* ("pitiless wretch") and *Ruaimill* ("muddier of waters"). The early episodes show promise. Cuaradh is put in charge of the health of the elderly and indigent and torments them by saying that if they cannot afford heating they should wrap up well. Siachaire is given the task of reducing the trickle of charity to the impoverished overseas, and travels widely for this purpose. Ruaimill devotes her black arts to disfiguring the English education service, such as it is, and adds a literal touch to the metaphorical meaning of her name by swimming as well in a "high profile" manner, presumably indicating a certain angularity in her stroke.

The innovation does not flourish. Perhaps the notion of weird sisters is too derivative; more likely, they actually lack a separate identity, merely reflecting aspects of Tachair's own tormenting, pitiless and muddied person. Poor Cuaradh, in many ways the closest to Tachair, with whom she shares a birthday, is written out of the script in a hair-raising scandal about poisoned eggs - so persuasive that thousands of viewers change their breakfast habits. The others decline into minor chatter like the impish *Guamach* (the "smirk", or Gummer) who provides a ghoulish light relief by force-feeding children, blaming everything on foreigners and arguing with bishops about theology.

Alas, viewing figures continue to slip, and the artful programme-makers prepare to bring the series to an end. This is no small step. To a simpleton, they seem to be building up to a Titanic climax - The Death Ride of the Nightmare Hag of Celtic mythology, perhaps, or some Valkyrie Ragnarøk from the Germanic or Norse. Not a bit of it. To see how the affair is managed we must expand on some material mentioned only in passing in the earlier study.

Rites of Uillseac

If you disregard the appearance of the Proto-MacGregor in *MacGregor and the Breaking Dread*, the first indicaton of the new course of fantasy comes in reference to these horrific practices. Readers will recall from

Chapman 40 the goblin figure of *Og* ("young", or Hogg), who becomes *Aillse* ("pixie", or Hailsham) when his father dies, mysteriously reverts to Og and finally becomes Aillse again when he "follows his father to the Woolsack" (*uill*, "grease", and *seac*, "decay"). Aillse's role is to guard the mysteries with incantations like, "the one thing about a layman is that he doesn't know any law" - as if one has to be a cobbler to know how to lace one's boots. Aillse has been celebrated in his younger days as a handbell ringer (a theme which runs like a tinkling cymbal through both series) and holds himself ready to comment on virtually anything. He thus cleverly emphasises the difference between Initiates of Uillseac, who may have their say about anything, and non-lawyers who should stick to their lasts.

These special qualities in lawyers are based on long-established ordeals of transition from the lay state, including feasting and putting on fancy dress before finally taking the Mantle of Uillseac with all its splendour and (until recently) bloodstained arcana. Indeed, there are those who see in these rites the survival of the practices of the Gaulish Druids, who were reported by the Romans to put victims chosen for human sacrifice in large wicker baskets and set them alight. The technologically advanced Romans preferred to kill people more efficiently in much larger numbers with the most modern weapons of their day.

A few of the principles of Uillseac are known to outsiders. One is that if the framers of a law do not say what they mean, the Companions of Uillseac will refuse to entertain any attempt by them to explain what they meant, but will decide the matter entirely by what they believe is the actual meaning of what the legislators did say, regardless of what they may have meant to say. This noble assumption not only spares the Companions potential embarrassment, but permits the flowering of a class of sub-initiates whose task it is to translate the intentions of the laity into the secret language of the Uillseac (cf the legal phrases, "grease the palm", "grease the wheels" etc); it is for this reason, for example, that anyone contemplating mortality is advised to make a will (*uill*) to put beyond doubt in a couple of thousand words that, to the satisfaction of initiates, the forms have been observed.

A second principle is that initiates are right and respectable, unless pronounced otherwise by initiates of a superior degree. For most of the time this is a harmless convention which makes for the suspension of disbelief essential to enjoying television. But it may slip into farce, notably in the sayings of the ancient Denning (*Deannag*, a "sip" or "pinch": a little going a long way). This gnarled and thewy figure, with a long peasant face and rustic voice, calls for the innocent to go hang rather than have the integrity of the System of Uillseac prejudiced in the public mind.

Indeed, the citizen is so hedged about and swaddled in all actions from the cradle (however defined) to the grave (subject to planning permission, and for the purpose of this passage "grave" shall be deemed to include "crematorium" and "action" to include refusal or failure to act) by these strange and unintelligible rites that a visitor from Mars could not understand how anything is accomplished at all. The system is ancient, with just the touch of lunacy appropriate to the legend of Tachair (herself an initiate of the elementary rites). Then, with a breath-taking quirk of fancy, Aillse simply

disappears and is replaced by a Wee Free from Caithness called Mackay.

This Mackay is an equivocal character. He removes the monopoly of Uillseac in certain fields and divides his own Church by witnessing activities of the Church of Rome in respect of a fellow-initiate of Uillseac. At the same time he is a jealous guardian of the *arcana imperii*, or what rulers keep up their sleeves, since that decisions openly arrived at would be subject to the whims and fancies of public opinion and the wilful shifts and indecorous expediencies of politics (from which, of course, politicians should be protected).

The Cascade Comes Back

While the law of Greasy Decay is thus being fortified and entrenched, Tachair casts about for other means of enhancing the performance of the poor by straitening their circumstances. Some fiendishly ironic scriptwriter comes up with the notion that she should honour the name of Adam Smith, the great Scots professor, by dedicating to him a poll tax, a primitive laying of distress on every citizen of a kind roundly condemned in his voluminous writings. The tax is described as a "charge", to distinguish it from other taxes and to stimulate the notion that something will be provided in return for it. To encourage the poor, it is ordained that those who are provided from public funds with a dole or pittance calculated as the minimum to keep them alive should give some of it back for the charge, so as to be in tune with their neighbours. To emphasise the dedication to Adam Smith, Tachair *introduces the impost in Scotland first*. The Scots, being a sedate and conformable people, pay the tax in sufficient numbers for Tachair to propose it to her uproarious and ungovernable compatriots in England.

In vain she and the Four-letter Man from across the western sea become involved in another distant conflict, in the manner of *The Smiting of Gealtaire*. Neoshalach Laochan departs, piqued by the activities of a rival for her favours, and Tachair has now only one of her original companions by her side, the phlegmatic and ruminative Howe, a Welshman. He turns out to be something of a sleeper. His is not a Gaelic name at all, but the prosaic Scots "yowe", a sheep. A commentator once described criticism by Howe as like being savaged by a *dead* sheep, a tasteless quip out of fashion since the reign of Queen Anne. (Queen Anne was, of course, dead. cf Sellar and Yeatman: *1066 and All That*, London 1935.) But Yowe is merely biding his time.

Meanwhile, cruising about the fringe of Tachair's retinue is the blond and brazen *Easach-tighinn* ("cascades coming", or Heseltine), briefly noticed in *Chapman 40*. He has distanced himself from Tachair for some years because he loves Europe more than she does. Without going too deeply into the writings of Adam Smith, but as another Welshman familiar with the umbrageous and disorderly practices of the English, he opposes the capitation charge and in sundry ways makes it apparent that he is ready to succeed Tachair if only she can be persuaded to take herself off.

The next exciting instalment in the Tachair serial, *Thumping Majority*, will appear in *Chapman 66*.

Kate O'Shanter's Tale
Matthew Fitt

Who'er this tale o' truth shall read,
Ilk man and mother's son take heed,
Whene'er tae drink you are inclin'd
Or cutty sarks run in your mind,
Think, ye may buy the joys o'er dear -
Remember Tam O'Shanter's mare.

Ye
ay, ye
ah waant a wurd wi ye

juist poppt in, duid ye
oan the wey hame fae wurk, wur ye
juist poppt in
fur a wee blethir, wus it
a cheerie chinwag, eh
a quick hiya boys tae the smithie an the millar, eh
an a wee hauf o hevvie juist
tae keep juist
tae keep ye gaun, lyke

ay
bit juist the ane tho
ay juist the ane
an a wee ane, mind
juist the wee, wee, wee, weeiest ane
an then ye'r awa hame
ay
sulky sullen dame an aa that ken
ay
gaitherin hur broos, sae she is
ay, juist the ane
gaitherin stoarm, ken
nursin hur wrath, whit
ay, juist ane bit
ay, nae bathir
ay
oh, ay

well, dinnae geis it, Shanter
juist dinnae geis it

ye cam in heir
fowre in the bliddy moarnan
an ye wur buckled
cuildnae staun
cuildnae speik

haverin a load ay keech, sae ye wur
tellin us hou ye'd juist
goat bak fae a ceilidh wi the deevil
an hou come ye'd seen viv lumsden's belly button

a bletherin, blusterin, drunken blellum, sae ye ur
whit a state tae git intae
voamit stens
doon
the bak o yir jaikit
werrin sumbiddie else's schune
how cuild ye be werrin sumbiddie else's schune
an of coorse
yir knoab wis hingin oot
the tap ay yir breeks
nae schemm, huv ye
an sei if ye'v byn oot wi yon hoor
kirton jean again
sae help me
ah'll chap it aff

an ye hud tae be seik
aa owre
ma bran new, deep layered
haun-med bi crippilt weans in kilbarchan
tender pyle carpit
duidn't ye

whit a state

ye wur that pischt
that yir ain voamit
goat aff the flair
an ran ben tae the cludgie
an spewed its ring
ah dinna ken

fowre in the moarnan
ye cam in heir
duidnae waant yir tea, duid ye
(ah'v hud chips)
slavin away since six this moarnan
a ten myle hyke throu the snaa fur fyrewidd
fechtin aff wolfs an bears an lions
(ah'v hud chips)
slavin away
sooth o the boarder spanish meatballs
orange ginger
an tatties
(ah'v hud chips)
romanoff a la lila, wattir chestnuts

an custart
ah hud tae sen the bairns oot
tae bolivia fur the fukkin chestnuts
an ye cam in heir
but ah'v had chips
an a wee dona kebab

an juist whit
in the nemm o the wee man
duid ye dae tae the horse
ma best brawest cuddie, puir meg
that wis the tocher aff ma ain faithir
ye'v went an broke it
ye'r an eejit, shanter
a fukkin eejit
ah dinna ken whit ye wur playin at
bit ye better fynn that tail
pronto

Who'er this tale o' truth shall read,
Ilk man and mother's son take heed,
Whene'er tae drink you are inclin'd
Or cutty sarks run in your mind,
Think, ye may buy the joys o'er dear -
Remember, remember, remember whit happent tae ma fukkin horse.

Matthew Fitt

Michael Begg

THE HEART sparrow pulse
My pulsing scaffold/leaning pylon/Industry of my heart

My life is cut
on telephones
and training of the heart

The wires that rub
along the length
of journeys of the heart

The voice is lost
in distances
with static of the heart

I lost my mind
and money
following my heart

My mother pleads
for me to turn
my back upon my heart

She hates the pain
that enters me
with movements of the heart

I am a slave
to memory
and those who move the heart

I only feed
on energy
to gorge my hungry heart

Within a thousand
lifetimes
I give to you my heart

Never am I
selfish in
surrendering my heart

I don't regret
the years I've killed
quarrying my heart

and though I'm poor
and ruined
I still hold up my heart

However long
I live here
I will empty out my heart

The carpet soaked
and bloody
with the debris of the heart

Advice for you with your nose at a wall, frozen by the shock of bad days . . .

FOLLOW THE WORD. AIM AT THE WORD

Trail on until you are lost and involved in being lost. Give the idle information, distraction is the flesh of the core just as flesh is distraction. Accept that your final order is for pain and cosmetics. Tie the ribbon to your closed door and hang a string of bells where the draught is strong. Twist all that is wrong into all that you fight for. Drag up the anchor from your page and lean your shoulder to the hull of each line, heave it out of the dirt until your voice is moving. The word will move and bend itself into an arrow. The word will whisper in air on its open journey towards the hearts of all good men who ever dreamed of playing with traffic. The word will survive through all that you say and do because you did not invent the word. The word hooked you and guided you to the net and carried you to the deck where now you dance, flexing your arms and posing as the greatest catch of the day.

The fisherman and the Blacksmith
hook and beat the
SOUL

Who ever said the soul could sing?
Who ever could believe
its aching for you, "baby."
There is no truth here.
The truth of the soul
is the pain of hooks
and iron furnace barbarism.
Here is the hammer,
Here are the nails,
Break me, little one.
Hunt for me in dark oceans
and draw me in on hooks.
Open me to the ugly music
of a soul not yet at rest.
Draw from me a broken song
with hammers and your fire.
Bend me when I'm beaten.
Lift me from red ribbons
and nail me to your foot.
I am yours, nail me down.
Walk on me, your steps
will raise a broken song.
The soul is not engaged
in slow and easy love.
The heart is not embraced
by tokens of your peace.
The soul is a beast
that lives on raw hearts.
It wants to eat your family
and torture you with longing.
The soul swims in deep water,
sounding for a mate,
wearing down its teeth
on the bodies sinking down.
The soul is just a beast
that cannot understand,
the beauty of the mind
or the passing of morning.
The soul is lost in the dark age,
and only knows the hurt
that it can bare and wage.
Its mediaeval patience,
burning with the candles,
at home amidst the furnace

as the black deep of the sea.
It lives on hearts
and wets its teeth,
when it can feel us moving.
It will not rise for music,
It watches just the pen,
Its only contribution.here,
When? When? When?
                    Take that, alleged soul singer!

IN THE WRONG HOURS OF MORNING

In the wrong hours of morning,
I come for my voice to be broken,
- for your dress to be open.

But do not let me sing,
For mine is a voice that knows nothing,
That, like a thief it has not stolen.

Smother my mouth lest a lie be spoken,
Push through me. I am now your ring,
Something flawed on your finger.

A token and gesture of paste,
Begging to be stone when you kneel with me,
Growing precious with each moment you linger.

It is here, the fruit of this new voice I taste,
And the truth of your word is set free.

(heartbeat)
There is a heart,
                Lie.
.There is a heart in the city,
                Lie forever.
There is a heart under the city,
                Lie forever breathing.
There is a heart that beats underfoot, in your steps,
matching your pace with a pulse in the city,
                Lie forever breathing
                at the mercy of stone
                dreaming of home
                waiting for snow
                Aching to turn
                and open your days
                In the heart of this city.
(heartbeat and snowfall)
                                    Michael Begg

Mungo Macaterick: The Evolution of a Lallans Poet
James B Caird

Among the poets who have resurrected the long-dormant muse of Scotland in our generation, and restored her to a new lease of life, Mungo Macaterick holds an honoured position. Though lacking in the occasional lyrical profundity of Hugh MacDiarmid, the cosmopolitan scholarship of Douglas Young, the plangent melancholy of Sydney Goodsir Smith, or the astute publicity of Maurice Lindsay, he has his own gifts. He has untiring industry, a constant desire to experiment with new media of expression, an almost diarrhoetic verbal fluency, and is perhaps closer to the soil of Scotland, above all to that of his native Galloway, than the others. He was born and reared in the little village of Balmawhammle, renowned in the seventeenth century for its loyal adherence to the Covenant, and in the eighteenth for the more mundane pursuits of smuggling and rum-running, since when, until the dynamic emergence of Macaterick, it seems to have gone to sleep. He is descended from the Macatericks, formerly a lawless band of robbers who dwelt in the wild, rough country that surrounds Loch Enoch and Lock Neldricken, and is dominated by the frowning cliffs of Merrick and the massive black barrier of Craignaw. Today its only inhabitants are the screaming peregrine falcon and the stealthy adder.

Macaterick's poetical tendencies showed themselves at a remarkably early age. When not yet five years old, he was sitting by the family hearthstone one warm summer afternoon dispassionately contemplating the old sheepdog who was scratching himself with obvious relish, whereupon the youthful Mungo was heard to declare in ringing tones:

> Ye puir wee dug
> That lies on the rug
> A doot ye're fashed wi' fleas.
>
> But then wee dug
> Wha scarts yir lug
> Ye arena fashed wi' claes."

These verses with their amazing metrical regularity, and the remarkably mature perception they convey of the compensations of nature showed surprising precocity in one so young.

For the rest of his childhood and adolescence, however, Macaterick was like any other normal boy; he did not "lisp in numbers for the numbers came". He played football, robbed birds' nests and his neighbour's apple trees, explored his countryside, and listened avidly to the gossip of the village worthies. It was not until his nineteenth year, when he was employed as a reporter on that celebrated newspaper *The Galloway Clashmaclaver* that he felt an inner prompting to express himself in verse. For months he had been reading Burns and his disciples. One morning, when his duties had taken him to the eastern region of his county, he had climbed the massive slope of Criffel, and was gazing entranced at the distant prospect of the ancient and royal burgh of Dumfries. Almost unconsciously he began to string words, phrases and finally whole lines together. They fell of their own accord into the verse form most familiar to him from his reading - the Burns stanza:

A Loreburn Leid.

Bien toon that i' the days lang syne
His coupit muckle yill and wine,
Baith usquebae an claret fine
    Intill yir wame;
Tho quaeter noo, ye'll nivir tine
    Yir unco fame.

For ower yir aunccient causay stanes
Kenspeckle fowk hae played as weans,
An in yir kirkyaird lig the banes
    O mony a yin
That glorifiet wi' his brains
    Baith kith an kin.

Aft in my ingyne I hae hent
Auld farrant howffs that Rabbie kent,
An aft at times an antrin sklent
    O' bygone days
His garred me scrieve i' guid black prent
    Yir mead o' praise.

Guid neebors aa', whire'er ye won,
At Heathha' or i' Maxwellton,
Or i' the closes round the TRON,
    A mean the steeple,
The sun abune his ne'er shone on
    A brawer people.

Now, apart from a few archaisms, this was straightforward, conventional, intelligible Scots verse, and it was published in the *Clashmaclaver*, among whose readers it received its due mead of approbation. But the archaisms proved to be Mungo's poetical salvation. A copy of the *Clashmaclaver* by devious means reached the hand of Malachi MacPartan, one of the leaders of the Lallans movement in verse. MacPartan wrote to Mungo, praising his work with reservations, and urging him to enrich his use of Lallans, to read deeply in the works of himself, and to go back to Dunbar, not the Dunbar of the "Golden Targe" but the makar of the scurrilous flytings and the grosser parts of "The Twa Meriit Wemin an the Wedo". He also suggested that Mungo should acquire some familiarity with Gaelic, the language spoken in Galloway until about four hundred years ago.

Macaterick took this advice seriously, purchased a copy of *Jamieson's Scottish Dictionary*, and was soon plunged deep in the study of Middle

Scots and modern literary Lallans. The effect on his work was surprising; he
now despised the hamely jingle of the Burns stanza and consciously
collected archaic modes of expression, as other men collect stamps or
coins. The change that came over his poems may perhaps best be illustrated
by the lines that express his melancholy reflections on the occasion of
visiting Newhaven Harbour near Edinburgh. These were written in the course
of a visit to the Lallans makars of the capital. The night before Mungo and
his colleagues had imbibed freely at one of the numerous howffs frequented
by the Edinburgh literati. Perhaps that circumstance, along with the biting
east wind and the grey haar that rose from the Firth of Forth may account
for the character of the poem:

WERSH FORESICHT

A'm seik o' the fushionless, staucherin' cloods i' the lift,
An' the flichteran whigmaleeries that gar me drift
Noo here, noo there, at the pu' o' ma hert's fause tide,
Wi' nocht tae haud i' ma grup that's like ti bide.
A dicht the blatteran' rain frae ma bluidshot ee
An' grue at the luveless days A've ti dree.

Aiblins the maikless spreit o' randy Dunbar
Wis scunnert on siccan a day o' owerhappan' haar
Whan wi' chitteran' chafts, mair nor fower centuries syne,
He stude by the cauld grey firth and grued at the hyne,
An' thocht o' the dule o' this wanchancy life
As wi' blearit een he ettled ti glent ower ti Fife.

On his return to Galloway Mungo felt dispirited, prey to a nostalgic longing for the lights and literary companionship of the Capital. He produced
one lugubrious poem after another - all dealing with Edinburgh, its literary
life and associations, and sent them to MacPartan. At length the great man
replied, and in the course of his letter astonished Mungo by saying, "You
have gone off the rails. Your Lallans is thicker and deeper, but you have lost
your grip of actuality, and your work is becoming purely derivative. Leave
urban verse to Sydney and me; you must knit yourself closer to the Galloway
soil. Steep yourself in the folklore and tradition of the province; get to know
intimately every stone and blade of grass. And before you can understand
Galloway, you must delve into the Celtic and pre-Celtic background of
Scotland and Europe; you must go even further back, to the dawn of Indo-
European thought in the forests of the Himalayas."

There followed a lengthy list of books to read which included the
Upanishads, the Bhagavad-Gita, the Chronicles of Eri, the Red Branch
epics, the Norse Eddas, Vico's *Scienza Nuova*, the *Chanson de Roland*, the
Mabinogion, Marx's Capital, Douglas's Social Credit, *Carmina Gadelica*, the
Birlinn of Clanranald, the Praise of Ben Dorain, the Complaynte of Scotland
and *Finnegans Wake*.

Although at first disheartened, Mungo ploughed doggedly through all
these volumes and emerged a real Gallovidian Pict. True that his language
was still Lallans, but he had begun the serious study of Gaelic, and enriched

his work with a generous sprinkling of the Gaelic place names in which the district abounds. His interest in folklore emerges very strongly in the following work which is the first expression of the mature Macaterick, and indicates in what manner he had resolved his inner conflicts:

THE BOGLE O' GLENKENS - A GALLOWA RHAPSODIE

"The bogle kythed atour the mirk." (Old song.)

By nichtertale I sat ma lane
Upon a muckle harsk roun' stane
Beside the gray wa's o' the kirk
Aneath a lanely souchan' birk.
Nae mair kenspeckle kirk wis biggit
At Balmaclellen or Whinnieligate.
Twas that wae hour whan sunbeams sklent
An' cuddies loup atour the bent,
Whan ferlies kythe in antrin places
An' fleg us wi' thir weird grimaces,
Whan ghaists an' goblins aft appear
An' lanely rides the dreid nicht-mear.
For hours ma wearit pow I'd cloutit
An' wi' ma ingyne's gruntle routit -
Aa day in Jamieson I'd socht
Braw phrases for the blad I'd wrocht
O' Pictish makars an' the licht
They thraw on Alba's waefu' plicht.
Nae use. Ma hert was lourd an' laich,
Whan aa at yince an eldritch skraich
Garred me shak an' stert an' trummle
As though the bour trees wi' a rummle
A bogle gaed galumphin' by.
The unyirdly hichts beyont Dalry,
Mulwarchar, Lamachan an' Merrick
A phenomene mair esoterick
Hae ne'er behald; nor nivir will
Benyellary, Muldoon or Meaul,
The Nick o' Buchan or Curliewee
Sic an ill-faured visage ever see.
The reid lowe frae his gloweran een
Wad blast the girrd frae Corserine,
The slavers frae his girnan jaws
Wad flude the dam o' Clatteranshaws.
His michty tusks wad sune devour
The muckle clints o' wild Dromore,
Or ding ti smithereens the cairn
That croons the tap o' dark Bengairn.
The crieshy tow that his heid theekit,
An' frae aneath his bunnet keekit
The darg o' forsters micht weel spare

An cleid the slape o' heich Cairnemuir.
Ti view an unco sicht sae fremit
The bluid wi'in ma breist wis stemmit.

On the appearance of this poem a few unkind critics remarked that
"Montes" (in this case the Kells Range), *"parturiunt et nascitur ridiculus
mus"*, yet it was hailed in some quarters as a work of high promise. The great
MacPartan, in his *Pictish Buikleir* signified his approval and singled out for
particular commendation the imposing roll call of Galloway place names
which supplied a Gaelic thickening of texture to the poem. The bogle too,
according to him, typified the approaching Anglicisation and American-
isation of the Scottish countryside and was a profoundly-realised poetical
symbol. The review concluded with a recommendation to the poet to
thicken yet further his Lallans speech, plunge deeper into the spiritual and
cerebral dichotomy of Scotland, and effect a synthesis of the hitherto
irreconcileable elements that composed the Celtic ethos. Macaterick,
heartened and inspired by this advice, resumed his philological researches
with renewed zeal, and never sallied out without a copy of Jamieson's
Dictionary under one arm and *Gaelic without Groans* under the other.

After months of unremitting toil, however, during which his Lallans
became denser and more impenetrable and his insight into the soul of
Scotland murkier and more obscure, he arrived at the great decision of his
life. Henceforward his themes would be Scots and Gaelic but he would free
himself completely from the trammels of out-moded traditionalism. Why
be "cabined, cribbed, confined" even by Lallans? Certainly use Lallans as a
basis, but there was no limit to the variations - grace-notes he preferred to
call them - which could be played. Why be bounded even by intelligible
language? A sprinkling of Lallans words would suffice: the rest, Lallans in
form, would be the creation of his own fancy, and would be evolved to suit
the emotional and intellectual pressures operative at the time of
composition. Accordingly, one evening, after an undigestible meal of
charred kippers and burnt toast washed down with a brew of strong dark tea,
when Macaterick was sitting by his open bedroom window, vaguely irritated
by the raucous shouts of children at their play in the street below, he took
up his fountain pen and began, almost unwittingly, "in a state of dwaum" as
he himself afterwards described it, to write the following verses:

Ye swarch an swamble ower the battergins,
Ma hinny houble, oh ma smorchie doddle.
But gin the goustrous nebs o' stechy plorts
Gilravaged aa the ootgans o yir leid
Ye'd crocht yir crashtus creel o mueardrie
An speir nae at Fingal's flummerie.

He rose from the experience dazed but triumphant, and spent the rest of the
night wandering on the hills.

No sooner was the poem published than it was greeted by a chorus of
acclamation. Here at last was the direction Scottish letters were looking for.
It was the fine flower, the veritable justification, of the Scots Renaissance. It
had achieved a splendid synthesis between the Gaelic and Lallans elements in

Scotland, while at the same time sternly repudiating the escapism and antiquarianism that had been the country's bane for so long. It was the exact antithesis of the Celtic Twilight school, verse full of a Juvenalian *saeva indignatio* and not too readily comprehensible. MacPartan himself, usually so ready with a convincing interpretation of obscurity, admitted that it eluded precise analysis but therein, he maintained, lay its power and significance: in these few lines Macaterick had subtly undermined the whole structure of society as at present constituted. The effect of his poem would not be realised immediately, but in time it would bring about a complete reorientation of the spiritual, intellectual and economic life of Scotland. He compared its powers of delayed action to those of a time bomb, and prophesied a holocaust of innumerable obsolete notions and antiquated values.

Shortly after this signal triumph Macaterick retired to a tent made of badger skins which he erected by the gloomy shores of Loch Enoch under the shadow of of the frowning precipices of the Merrick. Once a week he ventures down to Bargrennan with his pony, Finn MacCoul, to collect his provisions, periodicals and correspondence. The rest of his time is devoted to an intense and silent communion with Nature in an attempt to reconstruct by intuition the vanished Pictish tongue of this ancient province of Galloway. This is destined to become the only medium worthy of expressing the ideas, emotions and aspirations of the Scotland of the future.

Alastair Mackie

RAPE

Earth is fattening;
vigour surges
through the cells.
Everything raxes
upwards from the root.

A hog's back
of dense foliage
on the horizon,
where once were
wind-torn scrawny sticks.

A light wind
combs the barley's
whiskery acres.
The landscape's geometry is one
of wedges and lop-sided squares.

Green knits up
the monotonous quilt
of fields until the eye is
seared by van Gogh's
skyrie yellows.

As you pass in the car
you catch whiffs of the odour
of rape, somewhat between,
heady syrup, and later, death,
as I smelt mother in her coffin,

her body dressed like a bride's,
her hand stiff with rigor mortis,
and rising from her wedding gear
a corpse's stench that no
embalmer's ointment could dispel.

BURNS 2259

'I have raised up a monument
outlasting bronze, dwarfing the pyramids.'

The ringing boast of Roman Horace,
20 centuries have not wholly stilled.

What of Burns? What of his love-songs
his cunning ear strung to forgotten airs?

Will not the snows of future eras
smoor for good that lyric fruit?

His monument, a collector's item,
scratchy records of dead voices

in a tongue long since alien
in the blood and mouths of singers.

(We shall never hear from space
the horse gallop of Tam o Shanter.)

And Burns' suppers, an obsolete rite,
with its sodden fellowship,

its yokel drivel, its wincing jokes
the curse of Scotland and its shame.

I guess and fear his Scots
will be a palimpsest, glossed in English.

And his country? An ethnic ghetto,
a hospice for the comatose.

Translations by Alastair Mackie

JULY

The hoose is bogle-hantit.
He raiks aa wey. Hear his fit-faas
up abeen in my attic faur
the shaddas play tig.

Whit a steeraboot, the vratch:
His fingers are into aathing;
tiptaes to bed in a dressin goun,
nicks the table claith.

Disna dicht his feet on the door-step.
Draughts whiz into skail winds.
He birls the curtain up to the roof
in a blawy echtsome reel.

Wha's this ill-trickit nickum,
this ghaist and doppel-ganger?
Hmmm . . . it's oor new hoose-guest
in oor country holiday hame.

We let the hoose till'm
for his short bit holiday.
And sae he rentit oor rooms
wi his air o thunder-spates.

His duds are jobby wi burrs,
the fluffy clocks o dandelions.
He comes hame thro the winda sills
and his tongue niver devalls.

He's a toozle-heidit gangrel o the steppes
smellin o lime trees an gress,
beet-leaves and fennel
and the green whiff o the parks.

NOBEL PRIZE

I'm done for like a penned beast.
Somewhere, people, freedom, light.
Behind me the baying of the quest,
outside, no bolt hole for my flight.

Dark forest or verge of pond
or felled trunk of a tree,
my road is blocked on every hand.
It's all one, come what may.

My crime then (for so it seems)?
Am I a killer? A cut-throat brigand?
I moved the whole earth to tears
over the beauty of my motherland.

Yet even at the lip of the grave,
that day will surely dawn
when brutish evil, I believe,
the good shall overcome.

Boris Pasternak

THE INFINITE

Aye dear tae me was this hill aa its lane
and this hedge-raw that pairts fae the een
sae great a wadge o the ootmaist horizon.
There I wad sit and look and pictur tae mysel
toom airts withoot end ayont that forby,
and silences abune aa mortal ken

and the foonds o quaet faur for a wee
the hert faas lown. And wi hearin the wind
reeshlin thro yon trees I gang on comparin
this saft sough tae yon infinite silence;
and I mind on the eternal and the deid seasons
an this ane here sae vieve, and the soonds o't,
that my thochts are drooned in this immensity
and shipwreck is sae sweet in sic a sea.

TAE IMSEL

Ye'll lie doun for guid
forfochen hert o mine. The last cheatry
I thocht wid lest for aye, is deid. Jist that.
Fine dae I feel it's dwined awa inside mysel,
nae jist the hope but the desire forby
for aa the widden-dreams I looed sae dear.
Lie doun for guid. Ye've dirled lang eneuch.
Aa your steer's nae worth a doit,
nor the earth your soughin. Life is nocht else
but wersh an dreich, and the world glaur jist.
Weesht nou. Hae your last bit greet.
Maist fowks' weird is death. And nou
ye may geck at yoursel, Nature, the coorse brute pooer
that, in dern, rules us aa tae oor common doom
and the infinite bleflummery o aa thing.

                                        Leopardi

THE CRACKIT BELL

O the bitter-sweet o wintry nichts
by the spirkin puffin-lowe, to hear
the ting-tang o kirk-bells in the mist
and lang-time memories rise in the ear.

Canty the kirk-bells' lusty jow,
for aa its years, waukrife still and hale,
deid on the 'oor it dings its hallowed peal
like a veteran sodger standin sentinel.

My soul is craized, and in its fits o langour
when it wid deave the nichts' snell air,
its plaints are aften jist a croupit wheeze,

like the deid-ruckle o a wounded man
neth deid heaps aside a blood-reid lochan
that dees athoot a stir fae his raxed agonies.

THE BLYTHSOME DEATH

In the grouwthy earth fair hotchin wi snails
I'd fain howk a deep howe-hole for mysel,
faur I wid streek at ease my age-aul banes
and doze aff into oblivion like a whale.

Testaments and grave-stanes fair scunner me,
raither than prig wi the world for a tear,
I'd invite the hoodies to bleed their nebs
aa airts, owre my livin cadaver.

O worms, ye deef, reid and eeless cronies,
come see a corp sae blythsome and sae free,
sons o the mools, philosopher-gourmets

gang your fell road owre my anatomy,
tell me gin there be ae mair hell to thole
for this corp, toom as the lave in this deid-hole.

BLIN FOWK

Consider them lang, hert, yon ugsome sichts
like stooky dummies, jist a thocht droll,
frichtnin, kenspeckle, like sleep walkers.
God kens on whitna airts their blin een fall!

A God-gien sicht has quit their blank ee-holes
as gin they gaupt at some thing hyne awa.
Their een byde aye on the lyft; they never
bou their heids' wecht on the cassies ava.

They are the gangrels o the endless mirk,
blood-brithers to the silence eternal.
Aa roon them, Paris, ye skreich, bawl and smirk.

Blin-fou wi pleisure and brutality.
Look! I drag my feet forby, mair gype me.
I say 'Whit's blin fowk lookin there for them aal?'

Baudelaire

APOTHEOSIS

The lyft's fair hotchin wi bunches
o worlds reeshlin in space,
nievefu on nievefu braidcast
aa owre the face
o the cosmic silence and ilkane
sperkin awa dour and alane.

Doun ablow this unkent neuk
there's a starny fur faur ae drap
o licht's winkin and blinkin
dowie-like i the muckle gaup
o the galaxies - the maister pint
to the lave o the faimly jint.

Yon's the earth; and there's Scotland
like a wee blob o licht
faur somewey, a silly gype
bydes up late i the nicht,
a doitit starn, wi a bulb abune
for his frienly moon.

Jist look at this ferlie,
the braith on a gless,
t' the haill cosmic ongauns
a wheen stour, or less.
It's the globe in 's heid
he tyauves wi insteed.

Adapted from Laforgue

Translations by J K Annand

ES WAREN ZWEI KONIGSKINDER

There were twa royal bairns
Whase luve for ilk ither was keen
But they downa meet thegither
For water lay deep atween.

"Ach dearie, gif ye are a soomer
Then soom owre the water to me
And I sall kennle thrie cannles
Whase licht sall help ye see."

There was a fause nun that hard them
Wha lat on that she was asleep
She gart the thrie cannles be mirkent
Sae he drount in the water sae deep.

"O fisher, dear fisherman, help me
And I'll be behauden til ye.
Cast ye your net in the water
And fish up the King's son for me."

She tuik him in her arms
And kissed his bonnie reid mou.
"O mou, gif ye could speak
My hert wad be blithesome enoo."

She happit hersel in her plaidie
And lowpit straught intil the sea.
"Guidnicht til ye, Faither and Mither,
Nae mair sall ye ever see me."

There was heard the jowin o bells,
Wi gowlin and greetin and dreid:
Here lye twa royal bairns
And baith the twa are deid.

O BAUERKNECHT, LASS DIE ROSLEIN STAHN

"O laddie, lat thae roses be,
They're no for you.
And ye sall weir a nettle wreath
Aroun your broo."

The nettle leaves are sour and sherp
And stang me sair.
And I hae tint my ain true luve.
That hurts me mair.

It hurts me sair and gars me smert
Deep in my hert.
The Lord ye sain, my dearest luve,
I'll never see ye mair.

UNSER LIEBE FRAUE

Our dear leddy
O the Caller Well
Gie us puir sodger chiels
O warm sun a spell
Sae that we'll no freeze.
Let us gang til the inns
Wi a siller-fullt poke,
And skail whan it's tuim.

from anonymous 16th century German originals
J K Annand

Art on the Bottom Rung
Paula Fitzpatrick

Not a good day. That wee bitch, Laura, wanted watching! Only two weeks in the place and coming the madam already. The cheeky little cow. She'd get on all right. That kind was always a supervisor in two years.

Lexie went home seething. Turning into her own close, she nearly fell over old Mrs Kennedy's ancient moggie, huddled in the cold on its mistress's doorstep, hopeless of making itself heard inside. The cat arched its back and spat at her feebly.

Lexie spat back. Or growl-cursed. At any rate, some unfriendly and uncivilised sound issued from her throat unbidden before she jabbed the bell-push. She was already a flight of stairs away and unheeding by the time the old lady's cry of thanks came drifting after her.

The soles of her shoes whispered, "Bitch bitch bitch . . ." like sandpaper on the concrete steps as she climbed and each door she passed was an ill-fitting lid which let a little of the pot's contents leak out. Helen Biggart's new baby giving it laldy, the smell of curry and cabbage and bleach, childish arguments, television gunfire. Other people letting their lives spill into her space. Everything irritated.

Home, an explosion of noise and mess. Bags on the hall floor, crisp packets, jackets, the television blaring in one room, the radio in another. She marched to the kitchen doorway and hovered, tight lipped.

"Could youse not even put away your bags?"

Bill was on his feet dishing out dinner.

"Hiya, pet. How's it going?"

She persuaded herself that the homicidal haze through which she was now viewing her family was merely the result of a bad day and that the desire to mow them down in a hail of bullet-shaped words was due to spending the last eight hours in high heels. She dashed for the bedroom and with her feet in slippers and her toes spreading luxuriously into the sheepskin lining she managed to push the memory of her day slightly to one side and achieve a (slightly) stronger grasp on her sanity.

It came to her then. Women should live alone. A tower block of one room apartments with low lighting and soundproofing and NO cooking facilities. No smell, no noise. No other people's mess. Just endless tea on tap. And hot, perfumed baths.

She returned to the kitchen snapping off appliances as she moved and Bill produced her dinner with a flourish. A stew which she'd cooked the night before and which he'd dried out in a too-hot oven. She thanked him.

"Here, there's a bit in the paper'll tickle you!" He pushed it towards her, wedging a corner helpfully under her plate. She glanced. Saw at once the familiar face (there had been other articles over the years) and pushed the paper aside. She did not need this now. Not tonight.

"D'ye see who it is?"

She wondered how it was a man could be so immune to a woman's mood.

Did they get vaccinated at birth?

"Who is it, Daddy?"

One or other of the twins could always be relied upon to produce the right reaction at the wrong moment.

Bill retrieved the *Evening Times* and held it up to his three offspring. "See her?"

Under the heading: "South Side Teacher Shows Talent", a middle-aged female with a butch haircut and too-youthful clothes smirked over Lexie's table.

"Kate Millar. She was at school with yer mother . . ."

"She was at school with you too . . ."

"Aye, but she was *your* friend . . ."

"We were never all that close."

Bill's eyes shot skywards.

"Close? Ye were like bliddy Siamese twins!"

"What about this woman anyway, Daddy?" Debs interrupted.

The article said Kate was having the third exhibition of her paintings in ten years. Bill read it out loud, slowly, savouring it and the children's reactions, missing nothing, interspersing the reading with questions that were almost, but not quite, rhetorical. Waiting patiently for an answer when she had none to give. Teasing.

She held herself apart, eating the leathery stew with a calm air, refusing to be drawn into his nonsense. He became more outrageous.

He had it that both Lexie and Kate were 'after' him at school and painted a picture of himself choosing in lordly fashion between the two. Frankie loved it! He chortled and jeered and aligned himself with his father - a mock skirmish of the sexes. The girls, with little tuts and sighs and eye-rollings, took their mother's side, feigning annoyance but enjoying the game. Stifling giggles, looking to Lexie for a lead.

Lexie saw all this from a distance, saw her daughter's glances, felt them willing her to join battle, sensed their disappointment when she remained silent. Did they wonder how it was that women had no sense of humour? She seemed to remember wondering that about her own mother.

She didn't wonder anymore, anymore than she wondered if old Mrs Kennedy's cat saw the humour of its situation.

"Can we go and see her exhibition, Mum?" Gillian asked.

"Uch, when would we go? I'm working tomorrow," she snapped back.

For a second she was tempted to say, "Get your Dad to take you. He gets Saturdays off." Then it occurred to her that he might just do it. She imagined him saying to Kate,

"Lexie would have come but she's working. Got a wee part-time job now. Shop assistant. Nothing much but it pays the holiday."

And she could just see Kate nod sympathetically. And smile.

And Lexie closed her mouth and flexed invisible claws helplessly.

The clock saved her at last. The kids rushed off, the girls to get their dancing things together, Frankie to get into his cub uniform.

"Christ, you're in a good mood the night."

Bill was smarting under the failure of his goading to cheer her up.

She nodded.

"Oh ay, sure."

"Whit's that supposed to mean?"

"What would you care?"

Angry and bewildered, he got up from the table.

"Suit yersel'. We're off. Don't forget *you're* pickin' them up tonight."

She had forgotten. The first Friday after pay-day was the "lad's night out". An evening of almost religious significance for Bill. And one more stitch in the blanket of self-pity she was weaving around herself tonight.

She heard them go. Listened to their voices on the stairs, heard them briefly at a distance in the street below. She cleared up and returned to the table with a cup of coffee. Now that she had finally achieved it, the silence hung heavily on her. She was already sorry. The anger had boiled off leaving only a faint sludge of doubt behind.

She didn't like him going out drinking in a bad mood, or sending him out in a bad mood. He wasn't a bad soul when all was said and done.

She sipped carefully at the near-scalding coffee, reached out for the paper still lying on the table and pulled her hand back uncertainly. No, she didn't want to read. For a while she just sat, letting the petty humiliations of the day drain out of her, purging herself of the crippling sense of failure that had got a hold of her somewhere along the line. What was so terrible in her life after all?

Suddenly, she got to her feet with a little rush and moved across the cramped room determinedly. She flung open the doors to the cupboard under the sink, pulled out the waste bin, removed the bag of rubbish and set it aside. She went down on her knees and began to pull everything out of the cupboard, cleaning fluids, rags, bucket, empty jam jars, sink plunger etc. The lining paper was torn in several places and filthy despite being reinforced under the bin with newspaper. This she peeled off and scrunched into a ball.

She filled the washing-up bowl with hot water and a J-Cloth and got back to her knees. Flipping the cap back on a plastic bottle of lemon fresh Ajax she flung a practised arc of cream into the cupboard. The movement pleased her.

She leaned forward, putting the upper half of her body inside. Another flick of the wrist and a curving zig-zag pattern of Ajax climbed the cupboard wall. What price Jackson Pollock now? Flick, flick. She drew the J-Cloth over her graffiti, making grey-yellow clouds with the dirt. Something glinted dully above her. Twisting her neck, she looked upwards at the underside of the stainless steel sink, grubby with dust and splashes of grease. It cleaned easily. Smooth and satisfyingly contoured. She drew the cloth around the surface a few times more - just for fun.

When she returned her attention to the Ajax clouds, her rubber gloves had made patterns in the paste. Finger painting. She saw Frankie's face, covered in paint and pride, returning from nursery school not so long ago. The technique reminded her of something she had done before in the art room at school. Paint on a worksurface? No, ink. Ink on glass.

She could hear Mr Franchetti, that tone he always used as if settling an argument:

"See, see? That's it, Lexie. That's the way! Come and see this, Kate. That's what I'm after. You've got to let yourself go a little. Enjoy your art!"

Lexie caught herself looking round for a piece of paper before realising with a blush that she couldn't take a print from a soap paste. Fool!

She checked her watch. Time yet before the cubs came out. She fetched a bag with old bits of used wrapping paper and removed two full-sized sheets. Both from the twins' birthday in August. Peach and grey swirls, that was Debs. Pink rosebuds on a silver background, Gillian. She was surprised at the effort it took her to remember what had been wrapped in the paper.

Strange how some memories were stronger than others. Sitting back on her heels with the wrapping paper on her lap she endured a 30-second kaleidoscope of Kate. Distorted, bright fragments from her childhood. Kate laughing, Kate at the shows in the Kelvin Hall, screaming on the twister, their two bodies pushed so close together it seemed as if one had to draw breath through the other. Kate crying because John Mullen had dumped her. Kate holding her up at the ice rink, everyone skating round in the same direction while the records played over the loudspeaker. The voice of that girl singer - not Lulu, the other one - booming,

"Walkin' back to happy-i-neh-eh-ess,
Woah-bye oh yeah oh yeah,
Said goodbye to lone-li-neh-eh-ess,
Woah-bye oh yeah oh yeah,
Set asi-de,
Foolish pri-de . . .

Siamese twins? Perhaps they had been close. It had been a funny friendship. They were nothing alike. She had always known Kate would get on, everybody had known that. Kate was full of go, always laughing, always up to something, a bit cheeky but everybody liked her, even the teachers.

She would go to Kate's exhibition, she decided. She could go on Tuesday. Gillian had an appointment with the dentist. She could go afterwards. Yes, she could take Gillian with her, go straight from the dentist. Introduce her. Say "Hello, Kate. This is my daughter."

She glanced at her watch again. Hurry now. With neat, deft movements, she measured, folded and laid the paper in place, smoothing it into the corners. She sorted through the heap of objects around her, discarding some, wiping others. She put them back into the cupboard, careful rows in logical order, carpet shampoo, turps and empty jars at the back, brillo pads and soda crystals to the front. She assessed her handiwork and was satisfied. Order out of chaos. She put a new plastic bin-liner into the bin.

Finally, she returned to the table and extracted the TV page from the *Evening Times* and saved it. She folded the rest of the newspaper open around the article on Kate Millar and carried at arm's length to the under-sink cupboard.

"Ka-ate," she drawled in a whisper, "do come and see my exhibition!"

And she laid the paper inside the cupboard. Then, taking the newly-lined bin, Lexie placed it squarely on top of the smug, grinning face.

And for the first time that day, Lexie smiled.

Paula Fitzpatrick

Angus Peter Campbell

THIS TIME AT THE FAIR

It is you again, overcoming beauty
with a web of grief and serenity.
                    Sorley MacLean - *'A Girl and Old Songs'*

It is you again,
overcoming grief with a web of beauty and serenity,
this time at the fair
where a thousand girls have danced before in the sunny fold
on wooden horses that were Agamemnon, Dante,
                    Dierdre of the thousand sorrows,
a thousand loves, MacBride's wife, the yellow-haired girl of Cornaig,
a thousand poems, the Handsome Fool's Margaret, Strong Thomas's Una,
a thousand kisses, Cuchulainn's Eimhir, and Grainne,
a ship called Cairistiona, black boat, perfect Greek,
silent, spirited, flawless
making, on the second thwart to windward,
for the green land of Clanranald, Uist,
the island of your barley without stint
where the bent grass of Gaelic is sweetest, a Chalum Bhig,
a m'eudail, rionnagan 's na speuran, rionnagan is reultan
returning and returning and returning
to that night when we stood on the brae of Trosaraidh
and watched the universal lights twinkling in the early sixties sky,
not they moved my thoughts,
not the marvel of their chill course
but now the kindling of your face, the miracle of love,
the golden riddle, the inter-lunar lords,
the memory of your face, o face, face, face,
turning and turning the widening gyre
and the horses at the fair going round and round
and you, Queen, Snow White, Cindermirrorinthesky
the fairest of them all, the fairest of ten thousand,
appearing like the dawn, majestic as the stars in procession,
your eyes the pool of Heshbon
by the gate of Bath Rabbim,
by the Big Park, by the river, by Loch Dunteltchaig
where we have walked by the incomprehensible ocean
ebbing drop by drop of grief, catching tadpoles, picknicking,
walking in the Highland air where the sea waves,
the grass waves, the bridges, the roads, the flags waving,
raising again, your big sail, you lit rope of hair
about my heart, a winding of gold, exclusive, particular,
a new captain, a new song, a new girl and an old, old song,
this time at the fair.

Aonghas-Phàdraig Caimbeul

AG ITHE SCONES

B' e seo Ard-shamradh Pròis a' Phrionnsa:
roimhn Iuchar,
bha e gairm athair mar Rìgh ann an Dùn Eideann -
thuit Carlisle, agus Penrith agus Manchester agus Derby:
mus do ràinig e Drochaid Swarkstone
bha Lunnainn, (tha an sgriobt ag ràdh), bun-os-cionn

gus an tuirt an duine còir, Lord George Murray,
"till dhachaigh".

Thàinig a chrìoch air latha fuar
nuair a chaidh mo dhaoine a mhurt le pròis, miann agus breugan.

'S iomadh bliadhna
chuir e seachad a' bàsachadh,
bogte ann am fìon 's anns a' chlap ghoirt.

Beinn Choraraidh agus uaimh a' Phrionnsa,
far a bheil am fraoch da-rìribh gorm as t-earrach,
tha cuimhneam air madainnean Caisg' nuair bha mi beag
's a' ghrian gu miorbhaileach a' dannsa os cionn na Beinne Mòir'
's sinne dol gu Comainn, ann an lèintean geala, geala, le faileas tartan.

Mo ghaoil àlainn, tha iomadh dealbh air do shon,
ach 's na làithean seo tha h-uile sian breàgha,
ag ithe scones ann an cidsin Cheiteig.

"SAY SOMETHING IN GAELIC, MISTER"

Agus b' ann ann am Port-rìgh bha seo:
balach sia bliadhna dh'aois,
's a sheanair, coitear a Bracadal
air a bhàthadh air a 'Hercules', Bhatarsaigh air a dhol à cuimhne

a m'eudail àlainn,
far nach eil seanair, bha a' chaitheamh, am fiabhras breac
                    agus a' bhuinneach mhor:
am measg osnaidhean a ghaire

cuimhnich Port-rìgh air an latha seo
's am balach ud,
a' foighneachd.

EATING SCONES

This was the High Summer of the Prince's Pride:
by July,
he was declaring his father King in the capital, Edinburgh -
Carlisle fell, followed by Penrith and Manchester and Derby:
by the time he reached Swarkstone Bridge,
London (so the script says), was in chaos

until his decent general, Lord George Murray,
said "go home".

The end came on a cold day
When my people were slaughtered by ambition, greed and lies.

He spent many years
dying,
soaked in wine and sad venereal disease.

Beinn Choraraidh and the Prince's cave,
where the heather really is blue in Spring,
I remember Easter mornings when I was a child
and the sun dancing astonishingly to the north above Ben More
as we went to Holy Communion in white, white, shirts
                              and a shadow-flash of tartan.

My first love, there are many pictures for your choosing,
but these days everything is very beautiful,
eating scones in Katie's kitchen.

"SAY SOMETHING IN GAELIC, MISTER"

And this was in Portree:
6 year old kid,
and his grandfather, cottar from Bracadale,
drowned on the 'Hercules', Vatersay forgotten.

my beautiful daughter,
where no grandfather reigns, there was tuberculosis, typhoid and cholera:
amidst the bonny sighs

remember Portree this day
and that child,
asking.

UIBHIST 1960

Air baidhsagalan,
chitheadh tu iad mìltean air falbh
anns an teas bhruthainneach, chritheach.

Strainnsearan
a' dearrsadh le cuibhlean airgid
's adan dearg 's pocannan uaine
's smeid mhòr anns an dol-seachad.

Fuaim na cuibhle, fuaim na cuibhle,
's a' ghrian a' bualadh air na spogan
's iad a' dìreadh,
's na rothan, 's na rothan, 's na rothan,
's na rothan:
bò ann an Gearraidh-na-Monadh.

UIST 1960

Cycling,
you could see them miles away
in the still haze of that Uist day.

Strangers
glittering with silver wheels
and red headbands and green pouches
and a lovely wave as they travelled on.

A soft hiss, a soft hiss
and the sun caught the spokes
as they climbed,
and the hiss, and the hiss, and the hiss,
and the hiss:
a cow in Garrynamonie.

Aonghas-Phàdraig Caimbeul

THE EDINBURGH GRAVEYARD GUIDE

Organise your own leisurely *stroll* around some of the city's most unusual *beauty spots*. Take a *wander* down the ROYAL MILE, from the CASTLE to HOLYROOD PALACE, and there is an *abundance* of historical *nooks* and *crannies* to capture the *imagination*, telling *tales* of the *famous*, the *infamous*, the *incredible* and the *strange*. None more strange than the *graveyards* of the OLD TOWN and NEW TOWN, and the *stones* which mark the final *resting places* of Edinburgh's *finest* and most *feared*. Enjoy the fresh *air*—expect the *unexpected*.

MICHAEL *T R B* TURNBULL

0 7152 0655 9 £4.95 160pp(illus)

Murdo and the Mod
Iain Crichton Smith

At the time of the Mod, Murdo tended to get into long arguments about Mod Medallists. He would say, "In my opinion Moira Mcinally was the best medallist there ever was. Her timbre was excellent." Most people wouldn't know what timbre was and Murdo had to repeat the word. On the other hand he would say, "Though her timbre was excellent her deportment wasn't as good as that of Norma McEwan who became a bus conductress on the Govan route."

Such arguments would go on into the early hours of the morning, and as many as eighty Mod Medallists might be mentioned with special reference to their expression when they sang their songs, as well as their marks in Gaelic and Music. Murdo would sometimes say, "97 out of 100 is not enough for a Medallist, since I myself used to get more than that in Geometry."

However he would add, "Mairi MacGillvary got 99 out of 100 for her timbre, though she only got 7 out of 100 for her Gaelic, since in actual fact she is a learner and was born in Japan.

Her expression, he would add, was enigmatic.

At one Mod he offered protection for adjudicators. This was a service which consisted of whisking them off to an armoured taxi immediately they had given their adjudication. For he said, "Don't you realise the number of threats those adjudicators get, not so much from the contestants themselves but from their close relatives, especially their mothers who have carefully trained these contestants for many years in expression, timbre, and the best method of wearing the kilt. No one has any idea of what is involved in producing a gold medallist. His Gaelic must be perfection itself as far as expression is concerned and must be taken from the best islands. Furthermore, he must stand in a particular way with his hand on his sporran, and his expression must be fundamentally alert though not impudent, though for the dreamier songs he may close his eyes. Now, a mother who has brought up such a contestant cannot but be angry when an adjudicator, who doesn't even come from her island, presumes to make her son fifth equal in a contest which only contains fifth equals. There have been death threats in the past. Some adjudicators have disguised themselves as members of the Free Church and carry bibles and wear black hats and black ties, but this isn't often enough as everyone knows that the Free Church doesn't like the Mods since they are not mentioned in the Bible. The Comunn Gaidhealach have even produced very thin adjudicators who, as it were, melt into the landscape when their adjudication is over; but even this has not prevented them from being assaulted. These mothers will stand in freezing rain outside adjudicators' houses and shout insults at them, and sometimes the more ambitious of them have fired mortar shells into the living room." Thus Murdo's "Adjudicators Rescue Service", known as ARS for short, was in great demand, and for an extra pound the adjudicator could make faces at frenzied mothers through the bullet-proof glass.

Another service that Murdo would provide was skin coloured hearing aids which in practical terms were in fact invisible. These were for turning off after the seventh hearing of the same song such as 'Bheir Mi Ho'. If the hearing aids were visible it would look discourteous to turn them off. So Murdo would advertise for people who would make skin coloured invisible hearing aids, and sometimes he would even apply for a grant for such people who had to be highly skilled and whose pay was high since they only worked during Mod times.

Another service he provided was special tartans for people from Russia and Japan and other distant countries. His tartan for the Oblomov clan was well thought of. It was a direct and daring perestroika white with a single dove carrying a Mod brochure in its mouth. Sometimes too it might carry a placard, "Welcome to Mod 1992 in Dazzling and Rivetting Kilmarnock, home of Gaelic and Engineering Sponsorship'. Indeed his sponsorship from Albania was the high point of his life, and he kept for a long time the transcript of the short interview he had with its president who at that time was being besieged by 300,000 rebellious people demanding more soap and toilet paper.

Murdo indeed became very animated at the time of the Mod as if he were emerging out of a long hibernation like the church at Easter.

He ran a service well in advance of the Mod for booking choirs into Bed and Breakfast locations and he further advertised a service for making rooms sound proof so that pipers could practice their pibrochs, one of which was in fact dedicated to him. It was called 'Murdo's Farewell to Harry Lauder'. He invented a device by which a piper could smoke while playing the pipes at the same time. He advertised this by the slogan "Put that in your pipes and smoke it".

But I could go on for ever describing Murdo's energy and innovative brilliance at the time of the Mod. It was as if he grew alive again, as if he vibrated with *élan*.

He was here there and everywhere, organising dances, selling tickets, raffling salt herring, giving endless votes of thanks, singing songs, defending the Mod in midnight debates, pinpointing the virtues of Mod Gold Medallists of earlier years and interviewing them in a special geriatric studio which was fitted with bed-pans, dressing up as a starving Campbell who needed sponsorship, writing short stories and sending them in under assumed names such as Iain MacRae Hemingway or Hector Maupassant. It was a week of glorious abandon for him, so much so that the rest of the year was an anti-climax and he could hardly wait until the Mod was to be staged at Gatwick or Henley.

Murdo's closely reasoned paper on why the Mod should be held in Paris was probably his masterpiece. He said first of all that many of the older slightly deafer people might think it was Harris and before they knew where they were they would be strolling down the Champs Elysées rather than Tarbert. Also there were a number of Gaels in Paris who had been detained there after the last football international, and some ancient followers of Bonnie Prince Charlie. Furthermore it was probably from here that the original Celts had come before they had changed from "P" to "Q". Also the word "église" was very like the Gaelic word "eaglais" and there was a small French religious sect called L'Église Libre to which Pascal had belonged.

So it was that Murdo was busy as a bee when Mod time came, especially with his compilation of Mod Medallists into leagues, headed by Morag MacCrimmon (aged 102) and by his selection of raffle prizes headed by his special editions of the Bible with a foreword by Nicholas Fairbairn, And a page three of aged schoolteachers for the Stornoway Gazette.

"I envisage," he told the press recently, "that our next Mod will be in East Germany. As a goodwill gesture I have decided that there will be no communists on the committee. I hope to see you all there, apart, of course, from representatives of the Press and Journal."

I should like but for the pressure of time to detail Murdo's other astonishing achievements, e.g. the year he won the Mod Medal himself by an amazing margin of 90 points, and also his epic poem which won him the Bardic Crown and which was called The Church and the Sound of the Sea. However, I have said enough to demonstrate that Murdo was by far the most interesting President, Secretary and Treasurer seen at the same time which the Mod is ever likely to have, and his creation of five twenty fourth-equals out of a total entry of twenty one was the most dazzling arithmetical feat ever seen and also the fairest.

His interview in Gaelic with President Mitterand was a sparkling performance when he countered the president's "Tha e fliuch" with "C'est la guerre".

I will leave him here at the highest point of his life.

Angus Martin

THE LAST WHALE

I am the last of the wandering whales,
the bard of a murdered race.
You hear, but cannot feel my song,
numbed by a long disgrace.

My songs are of joy and freedom still -
hear them go rolling wide
in the vast halls of the ocean
and down the roads of tide.

And as your flimsy tape revolves
I curse your wizardry,
a singer singing to himself
in the emptiness of the sea.

THE PLACE

The place; it is the place.
I have come to it at last.
Behind the window, a voice
that I remember, a mother's voice
singing to herself as much as to the child
drowsy in her arms. There is no man here:
her man is on the sea,
nowhere she has ever been,
and nowhere she could name.
Only the man-child keeps her company
in a house of silence, but for song.

Shall I go or shall I enter?
Would she know me as the one
she holds against her body now,
the fruit to the tree returning,
falling upward out of time?

HERRING RELICS (for Will Maclean)

What kind of gods are you
that you allowed your race
to be destroyed wholesale
by Man with his different brain,
his fear of drowning?
How come you never sleep, yet
succeed so well at dying?

There was a time he worshipped you -
finding little of you, he loved you all the more.
By clustered dwellings on the loch shores
and croft-houses open to the heavens now,
his rituals were performed: the weaving and roping
of nets, the caulking and tarring
of boats, and all to reach you. ·

But, see, his relics stand,
here and there the sparless poles
his nets were hung upon to dry,
stuck in the ebb, mysterious
in isolation and decay,
dreaming a new age of the gods,
the whales' homecoming.

GHOSTS

I have developed a strong attachment to the ghosts.
I love them, and let them come to my fire
and sit out their evenings, smoking and spitting,
waiting for night, that they may resume
the business of being dead.

They have not taken death
lying down - that much I understand
from ghosts. They crave activity,
and while we sleep are busy
visiting the emotional power-points

of their former lives on earth.
They plug in and are young again -
such visions that flock to them!
Be careful in your lives and do not
alter or destroy the power of ghosts,

which is stored mainly in buildings, but can also be
found in shady hollows of the hills,
in trees festooned with the invisible
streamers of children's laughter,
or on the bright shores of vanished summers.

Most of my ghosts were fishermen.
Their names are known to me, and one was in love
with a sister of my great-great grandfather.
They haunt the sea, in preference to land,
which renders them harmless in conventional

superstition, unless you happen to be in a boat
when night falls on a stream of power out there.
But they are powerless themselves, content to drift
over the shores that rang with their cries once,
as nets came in, seething with silver of herring.

They see distant lights, and the dim shapes of sail and hull
passing, hear the whale blow and smell her stink
on the wind, and gaze below to the phosphorescent screen
of the water, that flickers messages no longer clear
to them, for they are circling aloft, great silent birds.

THE CAPTAINS (for Tomas Tranströmer)

1

What is it out there that could
freeze you now, draw a sweaty film
to your palms and bug your eyes?
Only the living, by God, the living,
unmet, unfathomed to a man
where the inky hills are in their
old proportions and hissing ridges
of the water loom between the shores.
Who is out there? No one that you know,
captains, so cry in the night:
'What ship, and where bound?'
All bound where you are come from.

2

Loitering, aimless, at the Weigh-house,
a storm on the roof of the
bulking Christian Institute
beyond MacEachern's funeral cross,
a mediaeval intricacy of stone,
heavenward mystery uncommented on
over the clash of rigging and the lash
of harboured waves. The captains
pace in blue among the casual
knots of crew, pausing to train an eye
on the black well of the weather,
and almost - almost - saying: 'We'll go home.'

3

Receiving the captains into my house
required no preparation; they came
with the gait of men accustomed
to straddling water on the thin
comfort of drunken planking,
and rolled themselves politely through the door.
There was whisky for one hand and cake
for the other, and a window beyond
the clockface and the hanging light,
and they gathered there before the glass
seeing themselves reflected, and remembering
the outer space of wind and sea.

4

Let me shake your hands. Goodbye, captains.
Be careful out there, where you are bound.
Perhaps you have forgotten certain dangers -
fingers of gloomy shore and the sunken teeth of reefs -
and remember there are new lights. everywhere.
You'll manage, I dare say, but do not tell me where
you're going, or I may wish to go with you,
a passenger just - no skills to serve you with -
sitting below, hearing the tongues of the sea
and the creaking of the skiff's old bones,
a boy in the bilgy dark, hunched at a mug of tea,
far from home, my captains, very far from home.

Angus Martin

Jim Crumley

THE LATE SWAN

Leaned uncompliant
on the wind, stung
by the sleety weals
of its whips. May

- termagent witch! -
eggs on the tribe,
North! North!
with gasping misplaced winter.

Shetland's watersheets
are shorn of all swans
save this dishevelled
lone lingerer (too much

like me for comfort:
I too have overstayed
adrift and uncomplying
on shores like these).

Dare you shrug, swan,
at nature's bidding,
knowing swans depend
on being bidden and complying,

dutifully feathering
the tribal nest? Will you
still stir, swan, late
and languorous, forsaking

smoored Shetland
for the trysting fires,
or chastely stay
and marry my summer?

AT THE REDUNDANT CHURCH OF ST NICHOLAS

Nicholas redundant!
it was the speak
of all the saints,
parishioners drifting

shorewards from St Nicholas
on the hill
to worship at St John's
St Matthew's, whoever's

St was handy.
They smirked
(for even saints sin,
albeit mildly) and nudged

celestial ribs, winks
among archangels. Nicholas,
being saintlier than some,
rebuked them thus:

"At the Redundant Church
of St Nicholas
the door is barred,
the candles cold, but

the cloistering beeches,
the wind-preaching owl,
the anthemed thrush
still congregate.

The mortal remains
of Jane King, aged 26,
are glad of them
and have been since

she died in childbirth,
March 1, 1771. She,
uncanonised and coldly
summarised by sculptors,

was a greater saint
than I - I never suffered
thus for child
or faith. I find

still, useful employment
in daily blessings
- tree, wind, owl, thrush -
at the Redundant Church
of St Nicholas."

MUTE SWANS IN THE DARK

There is a fold down the back
of a well-assembled swan
which delineates in the dark
sharp as horizons. Swans lose
nothing of whiteness in darkness
but gather mysteries.

Ducks sidle by two-dimensionally;
moorhens merely merge. Not swans.
That spinal fold breathes breadth
not enough to convince
but just enough to unhinge
my old preconception of nature's night -

that no bird crosses the darkness
undimmed.

THE GARDENER OF VERSES

Louis your ghost
is everywhere among
the small crushed mountains
of the Pentlands.

How else explain
plashing footfalls
in the syke
where no foot falls?

Or wind's ambush
in Ravenscleuch's immortal
stillness - (a laughing
spirit's breath)?

Who else hovers
copper-kestrel-bright
overhead? Or leapfrogs
eyebright underfoot?

Or shifts all
quick-silvering things
the will-o'-the-whisperers
that stitch the seamless

and seemly garment
of the Pentland hills
a child puts on to go
gardening for verses?   Jim Crumley

Bill Headdon

AT BROWNSBANK COTTAGE 1990

"in death - unlike life - we lose nothing that is truly ours" - Hugh MacDiarmid

Ten minutes was enough and we've seen
your lane spill
off the Biggar road to its wake
of narrow ground, left untended in a rage
of shrubs and grasses, which break
the line of the hill
and weave a Whalsay stitch
that togs your cottage
in a year of rebel green.

We came to trespass
behind a fence sprayed
with the Atlantic's untouchable blue,
but could only imagine your table, self-made,
walled-up strong and rude
in the room's blindness;
books where they always stood,
a glass or two.

We left maddened by this June
day's notice of your absence,
but knowing it endures
beyond windows and doors
boarded up with plywood,
the flowerpots with last year's
blooms, eyeless in the silence
of a censored afternoon.

Better this desolation,
the rub and neglect of a ruin,
than a museum stacked
neat by unflawed hands.
As long as trees shape Scadgehill
and the plash of tides wash the Whaleback,
as long as young eyes see Tintagel,
Valda, your house still stands.

(Valda Trevlyn Grieve, Cornish nationalist, poet, born Bude 1906, died Lanarkshire 1989.)

Extract from an Unfinished Autobiography
Jim C Wilson

It was about six months ago that my wife suddenly left me. I hadn't expected it; she'd given me absolutely no warning. Just before it happened, I remember being wakened during the night by the sound of her crying. "Anything the matter?" I asked drowsily.

"Oh shut up!" she snapped in the darkness then began to sob even more loudly. The noise made it difficult for me to get back to sleep.

The following afternoon she telephoned me to say she was staying at a friend's flat and someone would be coming round to the house to collect her things. "Hang on a minute," I remonstrated. "Don't you remember the Youngs are coming to dinner on Saturday evening? What'll I do?"

"To Hell with the Youngs," she yelled down the phone. Then hung up.

Well! What else could I do but cancel the dinner party? I couldn't see myself handling the shopping *and* the cooking *and* the wine. And anyway, Margaret's absence would've been a tricky one to explain away; then there would've been a huge washing-up as well.

As soon as it sank in that it was me and me alone from then on, I got my days properly organised. For some years I'd been a freelance writer. I didn't make much but as long as I was sensibly economical I could get by. At first I missed Margaret's salary very much. She was a teacher and it was convenient to have the regular payments each month into the bank. However, with Margaret out of the house, changes had to be made.

I discovered that tins of Italian brown lentils were very handy: much cheaper than meat and of course you use a great deal less gas in just heating them through. I curried them, put them in salads, mashed them and concocted all kinds of inexpensive stews. What always bothered me though was going out for the shopping. Whatever time I went, the streets and shops were packed with women, mostly elderly. They always seemed to wear the same style of checked coats and furry nylon hats. Many pulled tartan bags on wheels. I knew what they thought of me: look at him; out of work; some of them nowadays refuse to work; bone idle. All these women didn't realise that I'm a writer, an artist really, and choose my own working hours. They couldn't realise that a writer has his shopping, cooking and cleaning to do before he can get the chance to tap out a few words on the typewriter. Sometimes I got so tired with household chores that I couldn't face sitting down to write anything. (It's useless trying to write when you're tired; you just produce inferior work.) That's something Margaret never appreciated: the time I devoted to keeping everything so neat and tidy for her.

She came home from her work one day, wanting to cook my tea. I was cleaning my typewriter in the kitchen. "Can't you do that later?" she asked. I could see she wanted a confrontation. I was angered.

"When do you think I'll get time to do it later?" I said, reasonably enough. She turned and walked out of the room. A few minutes later, through curiosity, I followed her into the living-room. She was staring out of the window into the back garden, her nose pressed against the glass.

"Margaret!" I exclaimed. "You're marking the glass. I just cleaned the windows on Saturday. Can't you be a little more thoughtful?" What did she do then? She burst into tears. Being understanding I let the matter drop and went back to cleaning my typewriter. But I can tell you I was seething inside.

However, I diverge. I wanted to tell you about going shopping. What I would do was rush out to the shops just after nine o'clock in the morning. At that early hour they were often empty and I didn't have to worry nearly so much about the elderly women. I chose shops where I served myself and just paid at the till before leaving. This was quicker and saved me from those tedious exchanges about the weather or being asked if I were on holiday again. After a while I grew to completely ignore the assistants and just put my money on the counter and picked up my change without saying a word. I bought my Italian lentils in bulk from a cash-and-carry.

Things ran smoothly enough until about a couple of months after Margaret left; that was when I began to experience the most disturbing dreams. I seemed to live all alone in a vast Georgian mansion and every day I had to clean all the rooms, polish the floors and beat the dust out of the tapestries which covered so many of the walls. Talk about rushing! I couldn't get the work done fast enough and there seemed to be some kind of threat, a pervading anxiety that something drastic would happen to me if I didn't get everything done in time. I always woke up with my heart thumping just before I got the last room completed; I'd feel sick with worry. It was a great relief to realise gradually that my real home was comparatively modest in size and much more easily cleaned than the Georgian mansion in my dreams which, if the truth were known, was grubby to the point of being unhygienic.

During my years as a writer I'd worked on short stories, poems and articles. I had one novel published. Unfortunately it ended up in the remainder shops, selling for 75 pence a copy. But I was proud of my novel; it described life on earth after a chemical war which killed off the whole female population. I was hoping the book would become a bestseller but my publisher was useless at publicity and failed to promote it properly. After Margaret's departure I decided to tackle something really big that would keep me fully occupied and engrossed. That's when I started my auto-biography. It's not nearly finished yet. In fact, it's still at the planning stage.

I built up an enormous system of index cards and files to make the project easier. I actually have one of the cards here to give you an idea of how I work; there are general headings which direct me to sub-systems that contain most of the information I need:-

CLARET -   favourite wine. See also SHOPPING (box 26)
CLEANNG -   see ROTAS (weekdays/weekends).
            Check cleansers under brand names.
CLOTHES -   see under DRESS SENSE and REGULAR RENEWING.
            Also GARMENT CLEANING.
COINS -   see under ELECTRICITY BOX, GAS BOX, PHONE BOX.
            Also HOUSEKEEPING PURSE (comestibles).
CUMIN -   used for Italian lentil curries. See also
            SPICE SHOPPING, JAR CLEANING (fortnightly).

48

Sometimes I thought a computer would be the answer to it all.

Being so busy with my autobiography, I had little time to socialise. Margaret and I were in the habit of meeting other couples for a meal or a few drinks. Margaret would talk about teaching or we'd discuss some television programmes or film but increasingly I'd find myself sitting silently, wishing it were time to go home. When Margaret left I suppose it was inevitable that I saw less and less of other people. In retrospect I think this was a good thing: I could concentrate on my work without any frivolous diversions and, anyway, I couldn't afford to go buying costly rounds in pubs.

I'd more or less established a new routine for myself and was reasonably satisfied with it when something important and rather singular occurred. I remember it was a Saturday evening because I'd just finished dusting the ornate railings on my staircase. To do this job thoroughly took me at least two hours on alternate Saturday evenings; I often wondered where all the dust came from. It was dark outside and I was tired so I switched on the television and flopped down on the settee for a few minutes' recuperation. The News was on, and *I* was reading it. No, I'm not kidding you. It was me reading The News. I didn't recognise the tie but there I was, in garish colour, looking very serious and reading out all the latest on the Middle East. I switched the set off and on but I was still there on the screen. I sat entranced for the next 20 minutes or so. As you could imagine, it made The News much more interesting than usual.

That night I slept deeply and, the following morning, woke up late. The sky was overcast and I could hear raindrops beating on the panes. I felt stiff but made myself get up. After all, I couldn't lie there wasting precious time with my autobiography hardly begun.

I switched on the radio. There was some light music which I drowned out with the whine of my electric toothbrush. I scrubbed my teeth for a good five minutes then examined my hairline closely. No visible change. I checked to see if the hairs in my nostrils needed a trim but they were all still short enough to be safely out of sight. I brushed my hair carefully with a parting on the right but that Sunday morning it occurred to me that this might be encouraging baldness so I laboriously changed my parting to the left. But it didn't look natural. I was about to change it back again when I became aware of the announcer's voice coming from the radio and realised it was my own voice. Incredible but there it was. I was introducing Manuel and his Music of the Mountains. Oh well, that's a turn-up for the book, I thought and, shrugging my shoulders, got back to rearranging my hair.

After breakfast I was about to get down to some serious autobiography writing when I remembered there was no rice left and I'd need some for my dinner; I'd have to brave the queue in the Pakistani shop. I put on my jacket and ventured out. The very first thing I noticed was that a dog had used my front step as a toilet; I made a mental note to clean it up at 2.30 pm.

The streets were quiet, presumably because of the rain, and the only other person I met was myself. We nodded to each other but didn't stop to talk. We each realised that the other would be in a hurry. With considerable relief I found the Pakistani shop deserted. I picked up a packet of rice and took it to the counter where I was very pleasantly surprised. I had taken over the shop, it seemed, and Abdul the former owner had disappeared.

"Are you in charge now?" I enquired affably.

"I certainly am," I replied with a smile, putting the packet of rice into a brown paper bag.

I paid myself and gave myself the change. Then a thought struck me. "If you're running this shop all day and half the night, when are you going to get your autobiography done?" I asked.

I laughed. "Oh I'll just have to fit it in *sometime*."

"Mind you do then," I advised myself. "Well, I'd better be getting back to *my* autobiography."

"Cheers!"

"Cheers!"

I left the shop feeling quite elated. Shopping would be a lot less onerous from now on, now that I knew the grocer so well. I might even get some discount from myself.

The rest of that Sunday seems more difficult to recall. I can't remember if I did any actual work on my autobiography but I know I got a bucket of water and strong disinfectant and thoroughly cleaned the front step. Shortly afterwards, I moved into the house on either side of me and became the postman.

I've already told you about the terrifying dream where I have to clean the Georgian mansion and never get it finished. Well, there's another dream I had. I only had it once. And it was during the day. I'll explain what happened.

I'd sat down at my typewriter to do some work. It was the day I cleaned the kitchen; this of course involved dismantling and rebuilding the cooker so, having done all that, I was feeling quite weary. It didn't use to be my habit to take naps during the day but that day I must've dozed off in my chair. (Nowadays I always have a sleep for a couple of hours after lunch, but that's another matter.) I dreamt that Margaret came back to the house and started shifting things around. I begged her to leave them alone but she just laughed at me. She changed the positions of the ornaments on the mantelpiece then went into the kitchen and jumbled up all the cutlery in the drawer. Even more aggravating was when she went round the house and tapped all the picture frames with her forefinger so that every picture was left hanging slightly squint. I wanted to stop her, to throw her out of the house, but whenever I tried to grab her, some kind of invisible force prevented me from reaching her. She went to my wardrobe. "Don't! Please! Not my clothes!" I pleaded.

She seemed unaware that I hung my clothes in a particular order so I could wear them out in strict rotation. Still laughing, she took the lot and threw them in a big dark heap on the floor of the bedroom then marched right across the top of them. I was trying to make up my mind whether I should try to get my clothes back into order (I'd need all the relevant index cards) or straighten the print of Beardsley's *Salome* which hung above the bed when I noticed something extraordinary was happening to Margaret's face. She was still laughing; however her voice had become deeper and was echoing hollowly. At the same time her features appeared to be melting, losing their shape, the way soap does in hot water. Her flesh began to drop away, quite neatly, leaving just the clean white bone of the skull.

The oddest thing of all was that I wasn't horrified or alarmed by what I

THE CHAPMAN NEW WRITING SERIES

THE GANGAN FUIT - ELLIE McDONALD

This eagerly awaited first book of Scots poetry lives up to all expectations. Ellie McDonald's combines the sharp, satiric humour of the north east with real affection for human nature. (£4.95 + 35p p&p)

MADAME DOUBTFIRE'S DILEMMA - DILYS ROSE

From bric-a-brac dealers to sirens, wooden dolls to migrant workers, these poems have energy, economy and striking imagery - from the winner of Scotland on Sunday's short story competition (1991) - £4.50 + 35p p&p)

STING - GEORGE GUNN

This Caithness poet & playwright grapples with the problems of modern society. His wild, anarchic voice pays no homage to convention and sounds a note of protest against all accepted things. (£4.95 + 40p p&p)

SINGING SEALS - GORDON MEADE

These poems evoke the east coast of Scotland, its geopoetic landscape, its shore-bound and marine life, and the mysteries of the seas beyond, all seen through Meade's keen and knowing eye. (£4.95 + 35p p&p)

AVOIDING THE GODS - IAN ABBOT

Ian Abbot was tragically killed in a car crash in 1989. A few copies of this book remain. A complete edition will appear next year. (£3.95 + 35p p&p)

BEYOND THE BORDER - JENNY ROBERTSON

"Jenny Robertson's verse has its beginnings in a deep well of compassion; and drawn up into sun and wind, each word falls bright and singing upon the stones of our world ... " (George Mackay Brown). (£3.95 + 35p p&p)

CHAPMAN PUBLICATIONS

THE DIARY OF A DYING MAN - WILLIAM SOUTAR

This unabridged edition of the final volume of Soutar's many diaries, begun on 4 July, 1943, four months before his death, shows him to be among the finest diarists of this century. (£5.00 + 35 p&p)

THE STATE OF SCOTLAND: CHAPMAN 35-6

Scotland: A Predicament for the Scottish Writer? A dynamic debate on culture in Scotland: language, literature, art, politics: Alasdair Gray, Alan Bold, George Kerevan, Aonghas MacNeacail, Iain Crichton Smith, T.S. Law, Joyce McMillan, Tessa Ransford, William Neill, George Davie. These stimulating essays are accompanied by challenging poetry and fiction on the same theme of the State of Modern Scotland. (£4.50 + 50p p&p)

from *Chapman*, 4 Broughton Place, Edinburgh EH1 3RX.

saw; my greatest concern was to restore order as soon as possible. Then the telephone began to ring, as it always does at inconvenient moments. I left Margaret with her head disintegrating over my clothes and rushed out of the room. My next sensation was of falling through the air until I awoke, extremely confused, on the carpeted floor of my study, surrounded by small pieces of broken glass. I used to keep a framed photograph of Margaret on my desk but it had somehow been replaced, after she left, by a particularly good one of myself. During my dream I must've lashed out and smashed it. I reckoned I was lucky not to have injured myself and felt extremely relieved at having got back to reality again.

I had an immediate urge to go through to the bedroom just to ensure that everything was quite in order but the phone was ringing, as it had been in my dream. I climbed back into my chair and nervously picked up the reciever. My voice sounded odd coming to me over the rather crackly line. Would I like to go for a drink? No thanks. Oh, go on; it'll do you good. Oh well then; a quick one, if you insist.

I surprised myself by agreeing to go but I decided I'd been spending too much time on my own and was worried in case it might have a bad effect on me. Besides, the dream had left me rather shaken and it would be good to go somewhere else for a change.

We met that evening at eight o'clock in a pub called The Jolly Judge. I'd no difficulty in finding myself and bought myself a pint of lager. I was surprised to discover that I had a part-time job there as a barman. The pub had a relaxed atmosphere but I was a little puzzled by the fact that there were no women present. I think I must've had quite a few drinks as the evening wore on but, instead of unwinding, I began to sense that something wasn't quite right. I wondered if I'd inadvertently said anything to upset myself because I looked terribly worried and uneasy.

It was shortly after that that everything becomes rather vague and difficult to remember. I can recall ordering another couple of pints then telling myself that I should perhaps move on as I'd clearly had too much to drink and was disturbing the other customers. I'm sure I argued; I've always been very aware of my rights but, obviously, it's well nigh impossible to win an argument against yourself. Things must've got a bit unpleasant because I eventually turned up in a policeman's uniform. I remember my right hand being covered in blood and after that there were echoing dreamlike voices followed by a black silence. Occasionally the silence was punctuated with the noise of closing doors.

The events I've described were harrowing in the extreme. It seems that I was heading for a complete breakdown; I'm glad it didn't happen and I managed to gain control of myself again.

I'm still writing, of course, but I've organised a much less demanding routine for myself; I can take it easier now. I wash myself and then there are meals, afternoon snoozes and, as regular as clockwork, the injections. Mid-morning is undoubtedly the highlight of the day: that is when, wearing my neat white coat, I pop in for a chat with myself.

Jim C Wilson

Thom Nairn

THE QUESTION OF ENVELOPES

Careful and real as a drunk,
A tin-can in the wind
Skittles its way down the street.
You know it's crushed and careering,
Point to tip to a round mouth,
Not quite cubed.

Erratic, staccato as a damaged bird, but hard
In the night's sound of low dry aircraft
Over stone-rimmed trees shaking out
Paper bags and birds like confetti.

It is mild and mediterranean, almost mediaeval,
Worlds fold together in the interstices of the light,
Folding like the wings of a shell
Reaching for fresh and new space
To hold, enfold and enwrap.

Cities go everywhere at night,
The sharp edges of empty office blocks
Offering blank and dank wedges against open space,
Resting on the moon's keen and sickled edge.

Lost voices slide and echo
On winds that don't exist,
Chasing hard on a world's incoherence.

So when rain, fast and warm,
Comes at the windows
There is little left to think of
But shoals and lost swarms of insects
In a quiet violence, inventing
New places to be.

ARTHUR RIMBAUD ALMOST IMAGINES JOHN DAVIDSON

Rimbaud sits dark eyed and rotting,
Stalking the streets of an old Paris night
He now hates, while still, always walking.

The world has crawled and
Bitten hard on him.

Eaten alive by Africa and
The still strange wanderings
And the wilderness
He knew only too well,
Too close.

Still has him-self in his mind,
Black image inverted, corrupting and stark,
Showing and seeing himself
Mirrored in a camel's eye,
Picked up and transceived
Through the wrong end
Of someone else's telescope.

And later, John Davidson
Is walking, out of time
And into the sea,
Rimbaud, walking still,
Skulking in a dark-room enclave
On the edge of that other
Stark and not too distant mind.

CHAGALL TAKES A FALL

Ice-slide, Bagatelle, Pin-ball, Night-slide.
Low stone and swerving city square.
De Chirico's ghost on a skateboard

Passing in silence, brush between teeth,
Arms outspread, eyes acute for clocks,
For Chagall on a mountain bike
Checking the sway:

Taking notes of smeared and bloodied leaves,
Gouged, scoured and scored
By cruising skateboarders boarding,

Offloading,
Wiping warm, soft and suspecting flesh
Over yards of flaying, grating stone.

And Pablo,
            As De Chirico dwindles,
                        Chagall falls off,
As perspectives run off the page,
Dry leaves wait for rain or cutting wheels,
Knows, as usual, he's on a winner.

                                    Thom Nairn

WANT TO BE
SOMEWHERE ELSE
THIS FESTIVAL ?
BE AT
THEATRE WORKSHOP

Magic Bob & Mr Boom (Scotland)
Sunil Gupta (England) Big Nazo (U.S.A.)
Contemporary Polish Theatre (Poland)
Mandela Theatre Company (Scotland)
Clyde Unity Theatre (Scotland)
Shinko Theatre (Japan) Elere Yoruba (England)
Fleur Howard (England) Terry Beck Troup (U.S.A.)
Volcano Theatre (Wales) Andy Munro (Scotland)
Aids Positive Underground Theatre (England)
Annexe Theatre (Scotland) Sieve & Shears (Scotland)
Three Women And A Passion (Australia)
Scottish Traditional Storytellers (Scotland)
Livestock Nine   Livestock Shorties

9 - 31 AUGUST 1991

THEATRE WORKSHOP 34 HAMILTON PLACE EH3 5AX
031 226 5425

*"The best performance venue at the Edinburgh Festival
Fringe"*
THE INDEPENDENT

Norman Cameron - Unacknowledged Scot
Kate Calder

Robert Gordon . . . stood before the mirror and deprecated his Scots face. He could not think why his face reminded him of Scotland. It was only a face, big-boned, hollow-eyed, much-lined from the nose to the mouth, bushily eyebrowed, cautious-lipped . . . he refused to think of himself as a lump of clay shaped in a set country, by a mother from Fife, by a father who believed in home rule and free will. He was Gordon the international breather, he was cosmopolitan Robert, the normal man. But staring into his own eyes, he began to think of home rule and a detached house in the better quarter of Edinburgh."

The Death of the King's Canary (Penguin 1976) completed by Dylan Thomas and John Davenport in 1940, is a spoof detective story in which the poet laureate (the canary) is murdered. Robert Gordon, a Scots poet, makes several appearances. The physical characteristics and the nickname 'normal' show this is a portrait of Norman Cameron, a friend of Thomas. Though the angst is presented comically, Cameron seems to share the dilemma of many Scots writers, especially those in London - does acknowledging Scottishness prevent one from having British, or more importantly, European credibility?

Since his death in 1953, Cameron has failed to be recognised as an important poet of the 30s and 40s, while his place as a Scottish poet has almost totally been ignored. In the early 70s I came across two poems by him in an old school exam paper. I enjoyed their poise and the creation in a few lines of a complete fictional world. The sardonic below-stairs narrator in 'In the Queen's Room' finally meets his courtly ideal:

> Now I am come, by a chance beyond reach,
> Into your room, my body smoky and soiled
> And on my tongue the taint of chattering speech,
> Tell me, Queen, am I irredeemably spoiled?

In the Scottish room of Edinburgh Central Library I found The Collected Poems of Norman Cameron 1905-1953) (Hogarth, 1957) with introduction by Robert Graves. I liked many of the 50-odd poems in the book; Cameron, whose life had included time in Nigeria, Mallorca, North Africa and Italy, sounded an interesting man. I was pleased to learn he was a Scot, but assumed it was widely known. Tom Scott and John MacQueen had included 6 poems in their 1966 Oxford Book of Scottish Verse, and Antonia Fraser's Scottish Love Poems (1975) contains the beautiful 'Shepherdess'

> Now it is late. The tracks leading home are steep,
> The stars and landmarks in your country are strange.
> How can I take my sheep back over the range?
> Shepherdess, show me now where I may sleep.

His poetry seemed well-represented in anthologies of Thirties and Second World War poetry. When, four years ago, I decided to find out more about Cameron, I was surprised how neglected he was in scholarly articles on his work. Many of the best-known writers of the time had written witty, generous tributes to his personal qualities, but there were two obvious omissions: a recent edition of his work, and any article considering him as a Scottish poet.

Norman Cameron, Collected Poems and Selected Translations, ed Warren Hope & Jonathan Barker, (Anvil 1991), rectifies the first of these omissions. Jonathan Barker, formerly of the Poetry Library in London, and Warren Hope, American poet and scholar, have a "shared transatlantic enthusiasm ... for the work of a poet whom both see as unjustly neglected." The small body of Cameron's work has been extended by Hope's uncovering 13 unpublished poems. Barker's introduction is a succinct, perceptive commentary on the poetry, while Hope's biography includes much interesting information, especially on Cameron's early life, which is not available elsewhere.

John Norman Cameron was born on 18th April 1905 in Bombay. His father John Cameron was a Church of Scotland minister who after being army chaplain in the Khyber Pass gained a civil appointment. His mother, Isobel Macrae, met John when he was a Theology student in Edinburgh. They corresponded for 15 years before she went to India to marry him.

Norman Cameron spent little of his early life with his parents, as he was returned to Edinburgh to the care of his widowed grandmother when still quite young. Martin Seymour-Smith believes that Cameron was at bottom "drivingly unhappy" and it isn't difficult to see why. His grandmother disliked him, and by the age of eight he was boarded with the Todd family where he enjoyed a brief period of happiness with 'Muzz' (grandmother of poet Ruthven Todd), before prep school at the austere establishment of Alton Burn in Nairn. He was a precocious scholar, and won a scholarship to Fettes aged eleven, the normal entry being fourteen. There Cameron felt awkward and out of place, proving inept at rugby, which formed the ethos of the school. (Two years ago when I visited Fettes, the Bursar, Dick Cole-Hamilton, phoned one of Cameron's contemporaries for me. "Not good at games," was this old Fettesian's only clear recollection of the poet after 65 years.) Cameron's father died in 1913 and his mother returned to live in Edinburgh, but it is not clear whether he was a boarder or a day-boy at Fettes.

W C Sellar, later the co-author of *1066 And All That*, was a young teacher and became a life-long friend. WCS's light verses appeared in *The Fettesian* alongside the gloomier poems of his protege, Billiken. Some of these juvenilia, reprinted by Hope and Barker, are routinely adolescent. "My soul is some Leviathan in vague distress" begins one, and "What thoughts oppress/ the brain behind that monstrous lens,/ What wormy thoughts of death and dustiness" ends another. Yet the lovely short translation from Theocritus is obviously the origin of 'Shepherdess', quoted earlier:

> But here beneath the shadow of this rock
> I'll lie and sing and in my arms hold thee,
> Whilst there our sheep are grazing as one flock
> And yonder dreams the sea of Sicily

Despite the pedantic title, 'The Death-Bed of P. Aelius Hadrianus Imperator' is a masterfully succinct allegory in three stanzas, which ends: "A mouse, with timid inquisitiveness,/ Ran over the emperor's chin,/ For he heard no sound from the emperor's breast/ Of the small, dead mouse within." Barker quotes

Roy Fuller, that: "Cameron's clever style changed remarkably little from the interesting poems he published in the school magazine."

In 1924 Cameron won a scholarship to Oriel College, Oxford. A Bible Clerkship added to his income, but required him to undertake religious tasks. The autobiography *Myself and Michael Innes*, by fellow-Scot J I M Stewart recalls Cameron, whose "perception of the world's sadness at times seduced him from wholly temperate courses, announcing in the College Chapel that the reading would be taken from 'the Gospel according to St George'." As well as Stewart, Cameron's Oxford friends included W H Auden, John Betjeman and the painter John Aldridge, later of the Graves' circle.

At Oxford, Cameron continued to write and publish poetry. The first ten poems in the collection were all first published in *Oxford Poetry 1926* and *1927*. As in the *Fettesian* poems, classical themes predominate. Jonathan Barker points out that this "contributed to the rather formal and restrained style of Cameron's poems, one thing noticeably setting them apart from the work of his Oxford contemporaries." Other motifs and preoccupations are already present. The traveller-narrator who meets with a rebuff in 'Fight with a Water-Spirit' decides "No use to fight/ Better to give the place a holy name/ Go on with less ambition than I came." In *'Nunc Scio Quid Sit Amor'*, Love is a "most outrageous foreigner from whose savage smell I can't go free": "I fear you and I fear you barbarous Love/ You are no citizen of my country."

Cameron's taste for the classics links him with Robert Graves, and one reason for Cameron's neglect as a poet is the misconception that he is an inferior acolyte of Graves. Yet as James Reeves, among others, has noticed, Cameron "seems to have all but perfected (his style) as an undergraduate." Cameron did not meet Graves until he spoke to the Oxford Literature Society in 1927 - probably at Cameron's invitation. Graves then was 32, ten years older than Cameron, and at a crisis in his life. Still suffering from neurasthenia after his experiences in the war, he struggled to perfect his poetry and to support his wife Nancy and their four children. In 1926 he had met Laura Riding, a young American poet who was to have a profound effect on him for the following fifteen years, and on Cameron for a shorter period.

Laura Riding was 90 on 16th January this year (1991), an event marked by Robert Nye's birthday tribute in *The Guardian* calling her the "finest female poet of the 20th century". Few poetry readers in 1991 can claim to have read her verse, but she can still elicit this type of adulation. Graves worshipped her. Her beauty, her "uncompromising intelligence compounded with innocence and ignorance", above all her determination "to initiate a programme of education of men - starting with Graves" changed the course of Graves's life.

Martin Seymour-Smith, from whose readable biography *Robert Graves - His Life and Work* these quotations are taken, describes the tragi-comic events surrounding the Graves-Riding partnership in witty and awful detail. Cameron, now living in London, was an unwilling observer, and a confidant of the participants. A *ménage à trois* which included Graves's wife Nancy developed into a *ménage à quatre* when Riding fell in love with an Irish admirer, Geoffrey Phibbs. After chases to Ireland and France to retrieve Phibbs from the clutches of his wife, Riding jumped from a fourth-floor window ("Goodbye, chaps"), followed by Graves from a third-floor window.

This caused a terrific scandal. Within months, Graves and Riding had left England to live in Mallorca. Their need for money spurred Graves to write *Goodbye to All That* - now seen as a war 'classic' but planned as a best-seller. Cameron probably helped them with money, but didn't immediately follow them to Mallorca, taking up instead a three-year contract as education officer in Nigeria. Letters from there are quoted at length in Graves's introduction to the 1957 *Collected Poems*. The loneliness which beset him at school troubled him again as he was not in tune with the colonial mentality of the young British people he met. "Empire Day with its horrors is over. I thought of getting drunk, but couldn't think of anyone I wanted to get drunk with." Nor did he approve of the missionaries, even if "The Catholics are much nicer, though rogues too I expect. They always try to make us drunk. Their policy is better, too: they collect lots of tiny children and educate them and fill them up with Popery for a penny a week, whereas the Evangelicals try to catch them when pubescent and establish a snob-superiority and Christianity at very large fees."

Friendly relations with the Africans had their difficulties too. "The girls are most lovely. But I find you can't look at them . . . I had a sad experience when a girl I bought some bananas from made a gesture which I though was as sort of technical blessing. So I said 'bless you' and smiled at her . . . But she followed me and started to make a sexual demonstration. So I daren't smile at any African girls any more."

Cameron's sensitivity to language is shown in an interesting aside about pidgin. "I started off by refusing to talk what I thought was baby-talk to those blokes, and always used proper English. But I find that it is not baby-talk but a quite self-respecting language - English simplified - used by people from different districts when they want to talk together."

Suffering from fevers and missing his friends, Cameron gave up his contract after only eighteen months, and joined Graves and Riding in Mallorca where by now they were well-established in the village of Deya. For a while he threw himself wholeheartedly into their scheme for establishing a centre dedicated to the study of poetry. A legacy made him financially independent and he began to have a house built next to theirs.

But the atmosphere at Deya was strained. Partly because of spinal injuries sustained in the leap from the window, and partly her concern with "holiness", Riding decided that "bodies have had their day." Nevertheless, Graves remained devoted to her, and so, initially, did Cameron. Seymour-Smith records that Cameron told him that she exercised a "real fascination over (him). It was . . . a mixture of horror and awe, a feeling that at any time he might be overwhelmed into attempting to do something which would cost him his sanity and even his life, something he didn't want to do at all . . . But his Calvinistic mentality made him into an absolute devotee while he was under her spell." "When someone complained that Laura behaved as though she was God, he replied with gloomy earnestness, 'Maybe she is God.'"

The "kind of triangular situation which developed between Norman and me and Laura", as Graves put it, inspired Cameron's poem 'The Wanton's Death'. A woman puts her two lovers, a merman and a landsman, to the test, each having to exist in the other's natural habitat while "She to both quarters native, found them sporting." But eventually - wishful thinking by Cameron? - "Her relics lie on the sea-wasted foreshore,/ half-wooed, half-spurned by the land-tainted spindrift." The reality was more prosaic: Cameron donated his half-finished house and a sizeable sum to Graves and Riding, and was glad to extract himself from the episode with only financial scars.

In London, Cameron began possibly the happiest period of his life. He became an advertising copywriter with J Walter Thompson where his most famous campaign was for Horlicks. The slogan 'Night Starvation' was Cameron's. The strait-laced real advertising campaign was paralleled by a series of bawdy jokes and spoof slogans for 'Night Custard', a variant of Cameron's initials, which, Ruthven Todd recalled, could be "anything from the guck that gathers under beds to a kind of stew of squashed slugs."

Meanwhile Cameron's poetry was published in Geoffrey Grigson's poetry magazine New Verse. He first appeared in No 4 (July 1933) as J N Cameron, and he was a regular contributor from then on. (He became 'Norman Cameron' in No 9, June 1934). In October of '34, New Verse 11 was largely devoted to poets' answers to an 'enquiry' about poetry. This was sent to 20 poets of whom 10 replied. Cameron's replies are characteristically brief:

1. Do you intend your poetry to be useful to yourself or others?
    Neither. I write a poem because I think it wants to be written.
2. Do you wait for a spontaneous impulse before writing a poem; if so is the impulse verbal or visual?
    a) Yes b) Neither; first impulse comes from a vague sensation, as if somewhere at the back of my head.
5. Do you take your stand with any political . . . party?
    I believe that Communism is necessary and good, but I'm not eager for it.
6. As a poet, what distinguishes you from an ordinary man?
    Lack of interest in ordinary human, masculine activities, such as sport, learning and making a career. In so far as I am interested in these, the less I am a poet.

In 1936 his first book was published, and Grigson wrote an enthusiastic review in New Verse. The poems "are each an expanded image, an event . . . One need only enjoy them without wishing that they were bigger or better, as one enjoys nursery rhymes or folk songs." There Grigson also reviewed Hugh MacDiarmid's Second Hymn to Lenin - unfavourably. "77 pages of unvarying twitter" - though he made favourable mention of the pleasures of drinking with the author. It is not known whether Cameron met Grieve socially, but he did enjoy London pub life. He had many friends, and was generous in support of two interesting eccentrics. One, Len Lye, a film animator from New Zealand, produced several short films for the GPO unit which still seem fresh and original today. Lye recalled Cameron as "a long-legged walking essence of poetry himself with a dry humour of marvellous wit and sociability."

Cameron's relationship with Dylan Thomas developed from an affable pub friendship into something more complex. In 1934 Thomas recorded their fellow feeling as outsiders in London, complaining of the absurd behaviour of people who waited for 40 hours in cold and fog to see a royal wedding that they "should all be put in lunatic asylums. (Cameron) said that there was no necessity; all that needs to be done is to keep them in England."

It was Thomas who christened him 'Normal' as the apparently even tenor of Cameron's business life irritated Thomas. Cameron liked to tease the impecunious Thomas as a letter from Thomas to John Davenport in 1939 indicated. Thomas, hoping to put his sponging on a regular footing, wanted to get a number of 'sponsors' willing to pay him five shillings a week but "Norman suggested a bank account into which all sponsors could put a series of post-dated cheques." Thomas confessed himself "baffled". Later Cameron's annoyance with Thomas surfaced in an uncharacteristically bad-tempered poem, 'The Dirty Little Accuser': "Who invited him in? - What was he doing here/ that insolent little ruffian, that crapulous lout?"

Towards the end of the 30s Cameron began work on his translations of Rimbaud's poetry. He was helped by Laura Riding, who, with Graves, had left Mallorca during the Spanish Civil War. Cameron now felt "free" of her, and as she had a genuine talent for helping other writers with their work, their poetic collaboration seems to have been worthwhile. Probably the best-known of the Rimbaud translations is 'The Drunken Boat':

> As I proceeded down along impassive rivers
> I lost my crew of haulers: they'd been seized by hosts
> Of whooping Redskins who had emptied out their quivers
> Against these naked targets, nailed to coloured posts.

Anvil have republished the Rimbaud translations in a separate volume. It is good that they are in print again. However, I'm disappointed that the "selected translations" in *this* volume don't include a few of the Rimbaud, so that we had all of Cameron's best work in the one volume.

When war broke out Cameron's talents were employed for Government propaganda. He wrote a radio series *Kurt und Willi* which Graves claimed "was much enjoyed by Rommel and his officers in the Western Desert." Asa Briggs, in *The War of Words*, writes "*Kurt und Willi* was one of the most popular features; the dialogue written in Berlin dialect was slick and clever." This war work brought him new friends, among them the French exile Robert Mengin, who wrote "Norman had a gift for hospitality and was so gracious that one was warmed by the mere offer of a cigarette or a chair."

His talent for friendship was not matched by success with women. His first marriage to Elfriede Faust, a German, possibly contracted to obtain British citizenship for her, ended shortly before her early death from tuberculosis. His second marriage to Catherine de la Roche was, according to Graves in his diary, "Ill-omened". "Norman's wedding-day: God help him . . . cries of screech-owl last night reminded us of him." War-time separations and his affairs with other women caused this marriage to break up too.

Later in the war, his work took him to north Africa, Italy and Austria. He did not write many poems, but those which survive suggest attempts at experimentation and a loosening of his style. Sometimes this worked well, for example in the half-rhymes and long lines of 'Green, Green is El Aghir':

> Green, green is El Aghir. It has a railway station,
> And the wealth of its soil has borne many another fruit,
> A mairie, a school and an elegant Salle de Fêtes,

Norman Cameron

such blessings, as I remarked, in effect, to the waiter,
Are added to them that have plenty of water.

By the end of the war Cameron was suffering from depression which bouts of heavy drinking did not help. In 1946 he met his third wife, Gretl Bajardi, an Austrian journalist, while he was working in Vienna, and on their return to London, they endeavoured to make their flat a convivial meeting-place for Cameron's old friends. This marriage proved happy. Cameron worked hard during this post-war period on translations from Villon and a number of prose translations. Then a medical examination disclosed that he was suffering from high blood pressure. The deaths of his mother and brother Lewis, and the loss of many of his possessions in a house-fire further undermined him, and he died on 20th April 1953, two days after his 48th birthday.

Two years before his death he became converted to Catholicism, believing this would make his wife happy. This caused another quarrel with Graves who could not understand Cameron's motivation, thinking that the conversion stopped him from being interested in poetry. James Reeves, however, who saw Cameron shortly before he died, records how he discussed with Cameron a planned poetry reading at the ICA. Cameron "told me he was looking forward to the occasion, as he hoped it would lead to the establishment of his reputation."

This edition of Cameron's poems is a belated attempt to do that. Barker's introduction considers Cameron's poetry in relation to that of his peers, particularly Graves, Auden and Empson, and his influence on the later generation of Movement poets. This latter connection is made in more detail in Blake Morrison's *The Movement* (1980) in which he traces Larkin's indebtedness in 'Church Going' to Cameron's 'The Disused Temple' which also explores the problem of what to do with unused religious buildings.

Since it was unfrequented and left out
Of living, what was there to do except
Make for the door, destroy the key? (No doubt
One of our number did it while we slept.)

Cameron's poem, Morrison believes, "embodies that tension between reverence and irreverence which the Movement found so meaningful."

When reviewing the *Collected Poems* in 1957, James Reeves considered that "most of these would pass for contemporary in the magazines of today," and Barker concurs: "By remaining just outside the mainstream of both decades, Cameron's own work appears today less damaged by changes in literary style than that of some of his contemporaries."

Barker is concerned with placing Cameron in the context of English poetry. Is it possible to see him as completely out of that 'mainstream' and within the context of Scottish literature? One friend of Cameron thought vehemently otherwise. Geoffrey Grigson insisted that Cameron's "English, the English he spoke, the English he wrote, had no trace of Scotch accent or Scotch peculiarity . . . (He had) no country. How odd it was to see him inserted with national aplomb, in a book of Scotch verse." Grigson, as the comments I quoted earlier on MacDiarmid show, seemed to have little sympathy with Scottish writing. It is noticeable too that nearly all the descriptions of Cameron I have read begin by describing him as a Scot.

Cameron has one published poem in Scots, 'That Wierd Sall Never Daunton Me', probably dating from the late 1940s, written in ballad form, describing the trials likely to befall a man who woos a 'wierd' - a fairy or witch:

> Aye, marry, will she, boastful Scot.
> A kiss is not the fee
> Will gar a wierd come share your lot
> Like any other she.

Worse pseudo-ballads have been written! But the case for Cameron's being considered a Scottish writer clearly doesn't lie in his use of Scottish forms or Scottish materials. I'd like to end by suggesting three areas in which Cameron seems to have affinities with other 20th century Scottish writers.

Despite lack of success in 'That Wierd', Cameron, like Muriel Spark and James Kennaway, and even Norman MacCaig, has a talent for brevity, story-telling in miniature, and even macabre effects, which is like the skill of the ballad makers. 'The Compassionate Fool' takes just three stanzas to tell how the narrator falls in with his enemy's plan to kill him.

> My enemy has bidden me as a guest.
> His table all set out with wine and cake,
> His ordered chairs, he to beguile me dressed
> So neatly, moved my pity for his sake.

The end comes swiftly: "And even as he stabbed me through and through/ I pitied him for his small strategy." This is allegorical, and Jonathan Barker explores Grigson's comment that "a good many (of Cameron's poems) body out phantasies which are the community's as well as Mr Cameron's." Edwin Muir, who shared Cameron's liking for classical subjects, was also interested in the fantasies of the community. Cameron's poem 'The Invader', with its description of an unnamed enemy despoiling an unnamed country recalls Muir's 'The Good Town' both in its subject and in its use of a first person plural narrator 'we'. (This is a feature of several of Cameron's and of Muir's poems.)

> Our shops and farms wide open lie;
> Still the invader feels a lack:
> Disquiet whets his gluttony
> For what he may not carry back.
>
> He prowls about in search of wealth
> But has no skill to recognise
> Our things of worth: we need no stealth
> To mask them from his pauper's eyes.

'The Invader' was dedicated to Cameron's friend, Robert Mengin, exiled from France, and like Muir's poem, commented on the Nazi invasion of European cultures. Despite his living much of his life in London, Cameron's interests were not centred on the English literary establishment. His friendships, his travels and his breadth of interests all indicate that (in the best Scottish tradition of Henryson, Burns and MacDiarmid) he looked to Europe for his inspiration.

Kate Calder

John Murray

daith isnae

daith isnae
seein thir flooers
caad furth fae the bud

daith isnae
feenishin thon
muckle prentit romance
gotten fae the library

daith isnae
kennin hoo
yer diary joukit atween heid an fit
yin weill ablow the cloods
an tither sae weill on the grun

daith isnae
kennin hoo
yer yen fer sweeties
gart ye pit by sae mony pokes
in amang yer bits

daith isnae
kennin hoo
yer fear o no haein paper
fer tae scrieve yer kin
gart ye pit by sae mony leifs
in amang yer bits

daith isnae
kennin hoo
ye mairkit oor faimlie's dwyne
wi fadit cuttins
gotten fae the Scotsman

daith isnae
kennin hoo
fae thae crynin buds
i caad furth flooers

deith isnae

MASTODON MEMORIES

In thir auld hills
I see the muckle skulls
o mastodons cleikit
in a dub o black pitch.
In the howe o yon brae
I see the sockets o their sichtless een,

aye, an in the howe o the hill
I see a skelp o polished ivory
raxin doon til the valley flair.
In the tapmaist snab o their craggy broos
that ay haud the first an last snaws
I see the frostit pow o th'auld duin bull
ootcast by his kin tae daunner an howk
the tundra his lane forby
mastodon memories.

Ahint thir hills
in amang the riggs an dykes, haughs an howes
there are bits an bittocks o knocks an knowes
yonder a rickle o vertebrae unyokit
an a pelvis cowpit
yonder a riven cage o marraless ribs
the breith caad fae't
or a femur enn dichtit smooth
by the lang stravaigin stride
o the baggy breikit beist.

An as this bourach o banes
rives aa the fermlan roonaboot
or an ice borne rock, lang lairit
is by the ploo uphowkit
or as the river big wi the melt o memory
is a siller serpent, or lovers limbs
ower the dwammin haughlans fanklin
in spate we tak on lives lang syne,
fer as we sclim tae hichts
whaur tae the fields inby can niver rax
English is riven ay by Scots.

fuckt

an the boy says yince ye've
fuckt thaim that's it ken yince
ye've fuckt thaim, borin as
fuck ken, sae the boy says

saftly i beseech him
in the bowels of Christ
jalouse it possible
ye aiblins hae it wrang

fer as i grup my mate
wi the twae spreidin hauns
o the luve seik puddock
whae hauds on fer deir life

an fer three days, i ken
eftir aa beseechin
an jalousin's duin this
is aa tae life there is

again i beseech him
in the bowels of Christ
atween fucker an fuckt
there's nocht forby the fuck

MURDO AT MEGGET

caain furth the oars
caain thaim back ower again
alang the shooglin jyne
atween time past an time tae cam
on watter hainit bi a dam
fer slocknin Auld Reekie's drouth

caain furth the oars
caain thaim back ower again
atween Glengaber an Cramalt
hashit names o fergotten fowk
the goat glen an the cruikit burn
ma bairnlike gaelic
blethers in ma lug

caain furth the oars
caain thaim back ower again
the screich fae the pins
the slorrop fae the blades
an the skirl owerheid
fae the plover, the peewee
an the whaup

a Mhurachaidh bhig na creach mo nead
na creach mo nead a Mhurachaidh bhig   1

in ablow Clockmore
a score o faddom deip
nae liltin fae the clachan o Cramalt
but the auld yirth soughin her last
breithin oot a wheen bit air
that lowses itsel
at length in the lift

a Mhurachaidh bhig cia mheud cia mheud
cia mheud cia mheud a Mhurachaidh bhig   2

aiblins a wee boy'll
caa his finger fae the dam
an this hainin sib aa hainins
suin'll be gan throu
an the castle will soum again
abuin the Nor loch
an steam'll breenge furth
fae the inundatit locomotives
an daftlike names like Waverley
will no be mindit bi the rattan
the slater an the craw
whae'll inherit the yirth

*och bithidh glic bithidh glic
a Mhurachaidh bhig, bithidh glic* 3

(notes anent gaelic bird sang)
1: dinnae reive ma nest wee Murdo
2: hoo mony hoo mony wee Murdo
3: och be wyce be wyce wee Murdo, be wyce

BHA MI NAM SHIUDHE AIR SGURR EIGE*

I sat upon the Sgurr of Eigg
an saw that Rum was tume
an looked aroon an kent in time
that Eigg wad be sae suin

I sat upon the Sgurr of Eigg
an heard the lichthous soun
an kent or lang the only sangs
wad be on the singin sauns

I sat upon the Sgurr of Eigg
an saw the mill wheel stilled
its watter but a bit slitter
its leid sae thrang wi weed

I sat upon the Sgurr of Eigg
an heard the buzzards scraich
that gart the rabbits tae their scarts
like the clan tae their cave

I lootit doon afore the Sgurr
whaur yince the warld gied vent
an kent this place a rinnin sair,
a stoun in aa wir memrie's tent.

*a heilan saw meanin that gin ye plank yersel on the Sgurr of Eigg ye can see
an ken aathin

MR ELIOT SPEIKS SCOTS

chap chap
the blinman walks
the blinman stalks
noo an again fins an loses
the waa the kerb
whitiver he choses
fer a guide

braid adagio
the river breenges
atween lang wadin piers
frae bank tae bank
atween Westminster
an St Pauls enthronit
it spreid containit

raggit pavlova
in the violet evenin
offers this wey an thon
her graveflooers
frae hauf glovit hauns

dour sail o day
swees on heivy hinges
as the sook on moorit barges
or a buoy this wey an thon
tethert tae the river bed

noo an again
the doos swither an ettle
wheech an settle
syne awa in a fan o wings
as if chappin wi a lang white cane

in this unennin flit
atween bieldless places
in this ennless rammy
o forfochen faces
a knotless threid
like a fushionless fantasie
cannae thegither onythin jyne

John Murray

The Stait o Scotlan
Matthew Fitt

Sei lest weik ther, ther wus this guy settin i the middill o a play aboot wurking class Scotlan. An he wus juist settin ther an his wyfe wis fou o valium an the bairns wur greitin fur a wee bawbee tae buy sum wakky bakky, an ther wus aa thir eimportant pyntes bein med aboot poverteh an hungir skelpin throu oor lan lyk twa mukkil skelpin things an this guy wus settin ther listnin tae it aa an he wus heerin damn aa aboot Scottusch independence an him bein a gey strang nationalust buddie, lyk his faither an his faither's faither an his faither's faither's faither an his maw as weill, he wus gittin mair nur a wee bittie pisst aff wi the hail kerry-oan. Sae he turns roon tae the petit bourgeois playwright an geis him a guid haurd rap i the pus an he gaes back in tyme tae sei whut Robert the Bruce wus daein wi himsel these days.

Big Boab wus settin oan his lane i this mukkil toom castle, haudin the bluid o a spehdar in ae haun an the bluid o a nation i the uther whan in dauners wir hero, wha's cried Laidlaw by the way acause the playwright wis a richt eima jinativ kyn o chiel, an Laidlaw troops up tae the wyce aald heidyin an speirs him: "Whut dae ye hink aboot the stait o Scotlan?"

Weill, Big Boab juist raxt fur anaithir spehdar an seyd:

"Je n'ai ken pas. Je n'ai ken pas l'ecosse. J'habite dans un mukkil chateau, je mange l'haute cuisine fur ma denner, je me leve oot ma pit l'apres-midi, je joue un aafie haundy gemm de golf, j'ai beaucoup de sillar: mais mes mains, ils n'ont pas barkit ni mingin - jamais. Je n'ai ken pas l'ecosse."

Laidlaw cuildnae mak heid nur tell o whut the glaikit aald king wus haverin at sae he tuik the furst plane oot tae Pairis tae try an suss oot Robert the Bruce's crack an he ran intae this Danisch guy wha wus cryed Laertes an wus oot oan the randan wi a haill stramasch o his cronies an thai aa gaed til this deid poasch nae jeans nae fitbaa colours nite club bit the management refusit tae raccunyse Laidlaws language an the booncirs wur gein him hassul sae the boys fae Denmark aa lowpit in an ane o thaim raxt ane o the booncirs a richt ramiegeister oan the bak o the heid an a rammy stertit an kerried oan until the Frensch polis schaad up, thugs wi dugs an durtie big maschein guns, synepit the haill loat o thaim i the jyle.

This geid Laidlaw a chaunce fur tae discuss the meenin o nationaliteh an he turns tae his nuwe pal an spiers:

"Whut dae ye hink aboot the stait o Denmark?"

An Laertes geis Laidlaw a strecht luik an seys:

"Fukkin rotten."

An he gaed oan tae say that his cuntrae wus this wee dump at the tap en o Europe an that since the aald king deed aabiddie hud gane aff thair heids an ther wus this wee nyaff cryed Hamlet ir sumhing an he was knobbin his wee sustir an he duidnae lyke it no ane bit. An whut he wus gaun tae dae wus gae bak ther sum dey an tell thon bastart prince exaklie whut he thoacht o him, bit thon wus faimlie mettirs an he'd raither no speik aboot it in frunt o trooslach an tynkies lyk Laidlaw an the lave o the scunnirs i the semm cell. This gat

Laidlaw's dander richt up an he wus juist deliberatin caain the heid-bummin coof oot fur a duel ir whithir it wuild no be better if he juist skelpt his pus fur him whan in cams the jyle-keepir scoffin a mukkil lang piece an tells thaim that the Scottusch Erts Cooncil hud pit up the sillar fur thair bail an duid oniebiddie ken what the gairlik wus. Laidlaw duidnae ken what gairlik wus sae he spiers the jyler whan's the neist tren bak tae Kirkcaldy. Strecht awa the mukkil lang piece i the jyler's haun turnt intae a compact an bijou twa-wey radio an he caas up this guy cryed René an seys til him:

"Leissin aafie cairfou-lyke; ah sall sey this anelie wance."

An twa deys letir an afore he kent it, oor wurkin class hero wus takkin a bit stroll alang the links o a braa wee toun oan the Frensch coast cryed Dunkirk.

Yon wus sum dey. The saans wus hoatchin wi boadies, aa paddlin an splaschin aboot i the wattir an ther wus an aeroplane wi daft thrawn wings that wus fyrin bullits at Laidlaw's heid sae Laidlaw schoots oot a fyngir at the pilot an yammirs:

"Whut dae ye hink o the stait o Scotlan?"

An a mannie in a bonnie broon jaikit wi rosie chafts an a wyne an a cheesie kyn o bellie stapt rinnin fur his lyfe an chips in:

"Well, I think they're a jolly decent set of chaps. King George should be jolly well proud to be working with such a brave and sturdy bunch of sports. It's all those jolly little jocks that are winning this rotten old war for jolly England, you know. Jolly good show. Jolly well done. Jolly . . ."

An the pilot i the aeroplane wi the daft thrawn wings cam oot o the blae bore o the luift an drapt a big blak bomb oan his heid. Laidlaw duidnae ken if he wus gaun tae thraw his ring ir laach his heid aff sae he fleescht it doon the reid drookit saans an lowpit oantae a schup fou o boys fae Arbroath an the schup wun awa fae the clischmaclaver o the guns.

The schup wun awa fae the clischmaclaver o the guns an sayullt up the wurld, passin men i wee boaties wi Townsend Thoresen staumpit oan the syde happin tyme bombs fur sair immorul bit perfeklie legul insurance purposies, an sae the schup pit him aff at Leith an Laidlaw seyd cheerio an gaed tae luik fur the Erts Cooncil chuamers tae bethank thaim for helpin him oot.

The cytie wusnae itsel. Pilton an Muirhouse wus aa cuddies an kye an sum jokir hud pit a mukkil gret waa aroon aahing, but Laidlaw kent it wus August an kent whut lyke the fowk wha run the Festival an the Frinj wur - flagarie-lyke erty ferty dunderheids. Sae no baithirt at aa Laidlaw chappit at the toun yett an tellin the yett keepir wus he no aafie sairie juist bit he'd left his matric cerd bak at the flet, he gat intae the aald toun o Embro. An he gaed in an the streets wur gey nerra an live cous wur gittin slauchtirt oot in frunt o the shoaps an fowk wur flingin bukkits o shyte oot thair wyndaes aa owre the pevmint. Bit Laidlaw bein sumhing o ane aktor himsel kent fur schure that aa yon wus juist a play, a communitie drama an in twa-threi meenuts ane audience wuild appeir an fowk would stert bunging pennies aa owre the schoap. Sae Laidlaw nivver geid it a saicont thocht an he gaed oan up the High Street an he wus juist aboot tae speir sumwan whar duid the Erts Cooncil hing oot whan a man lowpit oot fraw the puss o a close wi a durtie gret Durtie Harry gun an blaad awa this soorfesst meenistir buddie wha wus settin in ane aald farrant kerrij an aa the peepul oan the street cried oot:

72

"Help ma boab, it's yon deevil Jimmy Mitchell!" *

Laidlaw kent fyne it wus Archie Macpherson bit afore he cuild oapin his gub this mentul aald wyfie swingin a stool roon her heid hud pit the fyngir oan Laidlaw skraikin til the neist soajir: "That's the verra fella, sur!"

Sae Laidlaw near keecht his breeks an tankt it up the close efter big Archie fur tae avyde the toun guard an a lang holidey oan the Bass Roack an tae esk Archie if he cuild no sei aboot pittan *Sportscene* oan a wee bit earlier acause the wyfe's muthir aye phones an spyles the saicont hauf.

Laidlaw run fae the licht. Intil the skelet o the aald toun wynds an coorts, beltin alang lobbies o guff an nyse wi the hootchin braith o the closemooths whuspurin saftlins intil his lug in a stramasch o fremmit leids an the ren was pischin doun fae a luift naebiddie hud sein fur yeirs an the fitsteps o the fittroops wus drummin loodir an loodir in Laidlaw's harns sae he nips intae ane Oxfam schoap an the couthie aald buddie heerin the bell turns roon an Laidlaw seen that the couthie aald assustant wurkin ther oan a voluntarie basis fowre nicht a weik an Mundeys if the bairns wur aff the skule, wus the deevil.

Nou Laidlaw bi nou wus gittin fed tae the bak teith wi the haill caper an stertin tae regret smakkin the playwright's jaa an that it wus high tyme he foond a phone boax an geid him a bell whan the deevil steps forrit wi his politeeshun's smyle an twa sheip fur eebroos an seyd til Laidlaw in a Meenistir fur Agrikultur vyce:

"Aaricht wee man, hou's it hingin? The nicht's the nicht if ye play yir cerds richt! Wee man, ye'v won the chaunce o a lyfetyme - the richt tae appeir oan the Bad Fyre Challenge. This is whut ye hae tae dae. Ye spier me threi quaistons - aboot oniehing ye waant - an if ah cannae enswer them ye win, an the nicht, wir ster prize is a romantik weik-en fur twa in Cowdenbeath. Bit, if ah ken aa threi, ye'r sowel belangs tae me, ya bass."

Laidlaw, fer flummoxt bi aa yon, duidnae ken whut the hell tae sey sae he havers til aald hornie: "Whar am ah?"

An the deevil gaes: "Heir."

An Laidlaw, no kennin the centurie ir nuthin, spiers: "Whut tyme's it?"

An the devil gaes: "Juist efter hauf fehve the nou."

An suddentlie Laidlaw, myndin the haill pynte o the story, spiers: "Whut dae ye hink aboot the stait o Scotlan?"

The deevil's scheip contrakit in deip thoacht:

"It's in a hell o a stait, wee man, an ken whut, yir sowel belangs tae me."

Jusit as Laidlaw was aboot tae keech himsel an the deevil awa tae eitt his sowel, the frunt dore exploads an in pyles the Embro toun guard an knee Auld Nick i the baas an whyle Satan's takkin a radgie oan the haill loat o thaim, Laidlaw duis a runnir oot the bak wey. Syne he's bak i the stoor an glaur o the Embro labyrinth wiooten ane idea whar he is, whut he's daein an stull nae clue aboot the stait o Scotlan an camin sair gleglie tae the conclusion that he wus totallie fukkin loast. Syne juist as Laidlaw wus hinkin it wus no wurth the bathir kerryin oan an juist as he wus hinkin aboot gaun an lowpin aff sumhing high he seis this fess that he kens that he schuild ken. An schure eneuch it's Archie Macpherson scootin oot o a tenement an disappeirin doon a mukkil blak tunnil. Intrigued, Laidlaw follaes.

The tunnil reeks o a million yeirs o foustieniss an the derkniss is thik as a traiclepiece. Ther's a laich fer-awa musik o pypes an battuls an greitan weans an the waas ur laachin laachin at ilka blynn gallus fitstep Laidlaw taks as he traipses forrit. An syne ther's a wee toattie doattie duddie o licht, the sehse o a flee an the schep o ane ee, glowerin at Laidlaw angry-lyke an growin angrier an angrier an beiggir an beiggir an Laidlaw's rinnin strecht taewarts it. Syne he brusts throu the mukkil bricht dusc an the derkniss staps an blae an whyte exploadi Laidlaw's puss an green gress rowes afore him furaye an he kens bi the wey ther's stane schelfs raxin up tae heivan lyk a coliseum an the wey ther's twa fitbaa poasts gawpin intae each anuthir's mooth, baith gantin naethin dauntit atour the kerpit o a weill-luikit-tae gress, that he's cam oot the tunnil intae Hampden.

Laidlaw heers the dunt o the punt o a baa an he turns roon an ther's a heefin mitretangotub skreemin at him fae the fit o Archie Macpherson sae Laidlaw chists it doon an bak passes til the son o pherson wha says: "Walcum til the stait o Scotlan." An kiks the baa atour the feld tae Laidlaw wha seys: "Whut ur ye haverin at?" An punts it bak tae the gret guru o industryall relijun wha seys wi the douceniss o a heidmaistir: "The fitbaa groond is the anelie arena o Scottusch ehdentitieh, ken."

- punt - "Shyte." - punt -

"Ay, it's ane echtie thoosan seatir incubatir fur yon dreme-lyke heid in the cluds flummerie o a hing scottusch nationalusm."

- punt -

"Shyte."

- punt -

Ootwi thir waas yon daft-lyke dreme dwynes intae noacht. Snaa aff a dyke."

- punt -

"Ye'r a bletherin skyte, pal."

- punt -

"Wheescht wi ye. This is the anelie pairlement o the wee masses, the anelie governament o bonnie Scotlan."

An Archibaldus, heich preest o the wee masses, dreibbils the baa tae the aij o the penaltie boax wi Laidlaw playin ruschie-in i the goal mooth an beig Archie seys: "An sei yon Scottusch Nationul Pairtie, its rutes ur i the middill class an kiltit lairds an romantic fules an aeyweys wull be, an sei tae the boys i Westmeenistir an Sanct Andra's Square, tae thaim Scottusch Nationalusm is juist anaithir poleetikul fitbaa."

An Archie drehves a peach o a left fittir richt passt Laidlaw's desparate ekrobatik lowpin dehve strecht intae the tap left pouch: a bewtie. an Laidlaw's leein i the jaas o the Hampden goal mooth, no exaklie in a Chryste-lyke mennir, mair lyke a pyle o shyte, an he duisnae unnirstan an he duisnae credit it an he wullnae credit it an he wullnae waatch *Sportscene* oniemair tellin ye that nou pal an aa o a sudden ther's pure hunnirs o mukkil-boukit soajirs poorin oot the holl whar Laidlaw cam in, hunnirs o the Embro toun gaird steamin oot the playir's tunnil an geesestompin swippert atour the haly gress tae clap the airns oan Laidlaw's schattirt sowel.

Wi a wan-wey tikkit tae the Bass Roack aŋ a sehze eleivun buit i the pus tae luik forrit til, Laidlaw gits aff his erse an maks guid his escape whyle the aald toun polis ur swaarmin roon MacPherson eftir autogrephs an loks o herr an aa that. Sae Laidlaw lossis nae tyme vacatin the premises throu an oot o yon Embro-Glesga express holl i the syde o Scotlan. An the licht o dey braks owre his fess an he's bak in Embro bit his mynde's stull blawin awa bi beig Archie's speik an aa he kin dae is stacher up the High Street. An heir is he no neer knokkt doon bi a Moadul T Ford, a blak boax oan wheels biggit pentit an sellt - nae dout - in Bonnie Dundee. Bit Laidlaw's no owre baithirt that his hunkirs wur juist aboot mangled an he's stull stacherin aboot glaikit an wabbit an spesst oot an ther's a mukkil stuschie o fowk at the frunt dore o the Embro Sheriff Court Hoose an ther's bobbies an wyfies an soliciturs an meenistirs an men fae the pehpirs an men fae the madhoose an thai'r aa jabberin roon the sheriff court lyk fleas roon a cou's erse an Laidlaw duisna ken whut the herr yle is gaein oan sae he spiers this polis: "Whut the herr yle's gaein oan, pal?"

An the bobbie seys:

"Fegs man, is it no the tryall of the durtie reid Red juist?"

"The tryall o wha?"

"Wha ye sey? It's a gey querr airt ye hail fae son if ye'v no heerd aboot the tryall o John Maclean."

An schure eneuch ther's a lood rakkit fae the crood an Maclean cams oot the court hoose an he's smylin an ther's bobbies aa aroon him an aabiddie's elbain an joukin tae git neer til him. An Laidlaw's puscht forrit lyk a fethir oan the tyde an he's soomin throu the fowk neerir tae Lenin's Soviet Consul fur Scotlan an ther's a quaiston growin mukkil an immense an massiv an it's fillin Laidlaw's brens an banes an ilka sinnon o his hert an sowel. An syne ther's a strang sway an the twa men ur fess tae fess, chaft bi jowl, pus tae pus an Laidlaw stuttirs: "Whut dae ye hink oan the stait o Scotlan?"

An Maclean's gittin hassul affa twa o his blae suitit maistirs an thai'r awa tae bung him intae the gantin mou o the meat wagon an John Maclean whuspirs til Laidlaw: "Tae hell wi devolution, son. Try revolution."

Syne the polis liftit him an loakt him in ben thair maschein o steil.

An Laidlaw stannin ther i the hert o Lothian seen that ilka quaiston, ilka buddie, ilka king, prince, polis, ilka fitbaa commentatur, ilka pretenschus an dodgie leeturie ploat devyce, ilka eejit, ilka majik tyme tunnil, ilka wurd, ilka braith, ilka pairt o the haill mentul dreme hud byn speikin til his Scottuschniss an that ilka ivryhing wus ther tae schaa that independence wus no a joab for coofs in kilts or whyte collar dremers bit a momentus dey's dark fur the hauns an sowel o ilka wurkir, sae Laidlaw gaed bak tae the play aboot wurkin cless Scotlan his tell atwein his legs an he geid the playwright wha wus werrin a stookie oan his jaa a poke o Cadbury's Roses an he tuke his pless i the gret republikan drama o the makkin o the furst socialust stait o Scotlan.

Matthew Fitt

Oonagh Warke

ROCK

Which of us now would dare recall
White horses scudding the September swell,
Black wings' glissade of a clean-swept strand,
The sea-grained wrack and driftwood
Scrolled by a fabulous hand?
Or Spring's high tide
Rinsing every action
Free of guilt's profane corrosion?

Our immaculate beginnings! Our Tacitean ocean!
How fast their guiding currents ebbed
As the boundaries of our beaches blurred,
Flooding siren-sung to a far horizon,
This dark unplumbed diameter whose compass
Will not turn on that hallowed poise we won
Between the gull above the water,
The water under the sun.

We're half-seas over here, my friend,
But together we can hammer
These split spiracles of sound
Until hooped by new-strung harmony
To that first fulcrum's gravity
Our recovered spirits swirl,
Our sea sick blood enthralled forever
By tide's great axis pull.

UNDER THE DOORKNOCKER

That's where, chief, I'm leaving this
As a talisman against the kiss
I do not want us both to miss
                    By being out
                    And not about.

But since you are here and I am not
(The ancient mariner to move his cot
Demands, o damn, a hand), o what a lot
                    Of fraught
                    Desire I send you.

And trusting still that cheek and beard will meet
And hands and lips and chest and thighs and feet,
Until I ring you, sweet, next week, accept
                    This rose
                    In lieu of throes!

GIRONDE

"Seagreen Incorruptible"! O bitter Robespierre
Had you been here when the tide
Broke over the rocks this morning,
Each wave as taut and finely wrought
As the starriest jewel in Louis's crown,
Turning, returning, then turning again
To capture the sun but give it back
In a million spendthrift rainbows,
Even you might have paid due salutation
To such amaranthine revolution.
Our own drowned honour has swept with Roland
Since the day your Weavers spurned his name.
Old man, they would have fished far better fathoms
Lining the strand than those dark streets of Paris.

TERESA AND TERESA'S HOUSE

You placed roses in my room to welcome me!
Those roses, one peach, two of the palest yellow,
Have long since faded but nights when I awake
To goblin spikes of fear, their petals
Still drift softly from the windowsill,
Subduing the dark angel of my dreams,
And then again I understand how rich
This consolation is, and give astonished thanks
That God should lay that iron rod so gently
On my shoulder now, redeeming the heart
I thought was spent. Petals brush my cheek
To peaceful slumber, until tears become
The dew of dawn, netting the blessed light
And the horses' whinnied greeting to the day.
The breeze plays band to the leaves
Dancing on the gravel and I know
That should blind Raftery's homeless ghost
At last come up this drive in all his regal
Scholar's bardic pride, raising the pheasants
To plump and startled flight above the poplars,
He too would find within these walls,
Furnished by such living grace, the hearth
To melt the icicles that pierced his eyes,
The long dark winters tumbling from the branches
In a flurry of sparks as he accepts
The proffered glass. A toast now,
To your good health and fortune, and to us all,
To the tenderness that teaches me to take,
Years late but not too late,
My way by the light of my heart.

A PLACE TO SING

Under the pole star
I see a white gull dive
To end a perfect arc
Where the wind's space
Bends for him to be
Beyond the dark
Embrace of a sea-wave's
Lace-sped glove.

Where does it go? It turns
To an undersong,
A tremulous burden
Of lonely words
That had no place to sing
Before riding on his aegis wing
To an air that's finely,
Finally, true and clear.

What's clear to us? We are
Apart, for only here might I be
Wholly, and where you are
Whatever breaks
Must break above my head.
O luminous echoes, abide
With me. The edge is all
I have of eventide.

Quoth the Budgie
George Friel

It was half-past ten at night in the peaceful house of an elderly schoolmaster and his childless wife. She was talking to her budgie, and he was reading. He looked up and complained.

"You pay more attention to that thing than to me."

He got a sharp reply. "At least he answers me when I speak to him."

They sometimes pretended to be cross with each other, to put some variety into a quiet life. But they were never in danger of a real quarrel.

So she went on talking to her budgie. It was in a big cage, mounted on a chromium shaft nearly as tall as herself, and the tiny bird answered obscurely now and again.

Mr Green returned to his book. He was getting a bit soured at the way his wife kept fussing over her pet. But he always tried to be patient with her faults. And after thirty years of uneventful married life, it would be absurd to start quarrelling with her over a silly bird.

She talked so much he couldn't go on reading. He put his book down and looked at her. He would never tell her, but it pleased him to see she had kept her figure, though her hair was going grey. She was still smart and graceful, and she had been his cheerful slave since the day they were married.

But now inside his bald head a crabbit voice was saying things he would never have said aloud. "Stupid woman! Baby talk to a bloody budgie!"

His wife took leave of the bird as if leaving a friend. "Good night, Riki."

The bird squawked an echo. "Night kee-kee!"

She wouldn't take that for an answer. "No, no! It's you that's Riki. I'm Nan." She tried again. "You say, good night Nan. Good night, Nan."

The bird tried again. "Night-nan."

She put the black cloth over the cage and lilted her words. "See you in the morning!"

Riki protested in a flurry of squeaks with the same rhythm.

Nan turned to her husband, eager to have him share her delight.

"Did you hear that? Riki said what I said! See you in the morning!"

She went upstairs, and when he was sure she was in bed reading her *Woman's Weekly* for half-an-hour before she put the light out, he opened the sideboard quietly and hauled out his bottle of whisky. He poured a dram, sat down to work at the desk of his bureau-bookcase, and stayed up drinking till one in the morning.

He was trying to compile a book of verse for use in schools. He had been vexed when a young colleague published a textbook on the new maths. He himself, twice as old, and head of his department, with an honours degree in English, had nothing to his name. He wanted to do something about it and show a young teacher that an old man too could get a textbook published. So he began collecting poems, and when his wife asked him what he was doing, sitting up so late, he told her, "I'm working on my anthology."

He wasn't making much progress. He muttered to the papers on his desk.

"It's a pity Nan's no help to me here. She's a good housewife, but she's not very bright. Poor Nan!"

Upstairs in bed, poor Nan wasn't feeling well. She had a sudden pain when she put the light out. She couldn't understand it, and it wouldn't go away. When she rose in the morning she looked so ill that Mr Green told her to go back to bed. Dumb and suffering, she did what she was told.

When he came home that evening, she was up and dressed, talking to her budgie. She turned to greet him, flushed with excitement.

"He was talking away to me there like billy-o! Isn't that right, Riki? You're my pal!"

Riki agreed at once. "My pal."

She gave the bird a dopey smile. Mr Green was annoyed. He spoke to her severely. "You should be in your bed. You don't look well."

She tottered to the edge of a chair and answered weakly. "I think you're right. I don't feel well."

But she wouldn't go back to bed till she had served him his evening meal and washed up after it. And even then she put it off for an hour, chatting to Riki. She stood beside the cage like a teacher encouraging a backward child to read, saying the same words over and over till he could repeat them.

She crumbled a fragment of a tea-biscuit on a spoon and moistened the crumbs with a drop of cold tea before she fed him. When he finished, there were crumbs on his beak. She wiped them off with a paper hanky and scolded him.

"Dirty face!"

Riki bounced back. "Dirty face!"

She wagged a finger at him. "That's all! You're getting no more."

Riki flapped and squawked. "No more!"

Mr Green lost patience with the pair of them. He spoke roughly. "Come on! Get to your bed, Nan!"

With a quick echo, Riki squawked at him. "Bed-nan."

Nan laughed as she covered the cage, but it was the twisted laugh of a sick woman.

Mr Green told her to go and see the doctor in the morning. She tried to argue. "Wait around in that surgery, with all those folk the picture of misery? Not me! I hate the place!"

He insisted, and she obeyed. She always did what he told her. But she had great satisfaction in telling him about her visit.

"A waste of time! I think he thinks there's nothing wrong with me. Or if there is, he doesn't know what. Stay in bed for a couple of days, says he. I can just see me!"

She made little of the days when her pain was bad, and made a lot of the days when she was feeling fine. But the pain came back more and more often, and one morning she had to stay in bed in spite of herself. She wasn't fit to get up and go to the doctor. The doctor had to come to her. He was puzzled when he came downstairs, and asked Mr Green if she had had an accident recently, a fall of some kind, or knocked her head against anything.

She had fallen downstairs a month ago, Mr Green remembered. But she hadn't hurt herself. He ran at once when he heard her scream, and she said she was all right. The doctor shook his head sadly, and said he would call again tomorrow.

Nan submitted to her illness as meekly as she submitted to her husband. She was more concerned about Riki than about herself. Mr Green was less concerned about either of them than about his own troubles. He stayed off school for two days to attend to his wife, but he couldn't go on doing that. He got a woman to come in, from ten in the morning till late afternoon, to look after her.

Nan wanted Riki brought up to her bedroom, but the doctor said no. Lying there all day with the bird for company she would only tire herself talking too much. She must have rest and quiet, and try to sleep.

Before she would agree Riki would have to stay downstairs, she pleaded to have him upstairs beside her for an hour. They spoke together, with Mr Green hovering around, and at the end of their dialogue she gave the bird her final instructions.

"If they're not good to you, you tell Nan, mind! Tell Nan."

She told the daily help what to do about the budgie, and told her husband where to buy the right packets of seed, and she said he must let the bird out of its cage for a while every day.

He was surprised. He had never seen it out of its cage.

As if admitting a guilty secret she explained. She let it out when he was away all day, because she knew he wouldn't like it flying around the room when he was reading.

Putting himself out in the morning with a slice of toast and marmalade, he missed the good breakfasts he used to get. And coming home in the evening to a cold collation left in the fridge by the daily help, or sometimes trying to make a hot meal for himself, he behaved with the dignity of a brave man who knows he is unjustly punished by cruel circumstance.

He was used to the comfort of seeing his wife coming and going about his house in perfect health. He was used to the pleasure she brought him when she entered a room, so mild and calm her accustomed presence. Her illness offended him.

When he went upstairs to ask her how she was feeling she answered vaguely, and asked how Riki was doing. She worried about him. "He must be missing me. He needs someone to talk to. Do try and talk to him, won't you? Please!"

He promised, but he was beginning to hate a creature he had never liked. He was hot and bothered every time he opened the cage. He watched the bird nervously when it flew round the room, perched on top of the bureau-bookcase, when it went over and under its cage but wouldn't go in. He was never at ease till it was back inside, and he had the cage closed. And when he sat down at last to his whisky and his anthology he cried aloud in vexation.

"That bloody bird! It's more trouble than she is."

For Nan gave him no trouble. When he asked if there was anything she wanted she always said no. And he didn't bother her much. He took a sullen pride in coping unaided.

But he soon wearied of his self-service. There seemed no end to it. It was only what he feared when the doctor said she would have to be moved. The thought of her in hospital depressed him, but Nan seemed past caring.

Left alone with Riki he thought of selling the bird. He hadn't the heart to destroy it. But since he hoped Nan would soon be home again, he didn't dare get rid of it behind her back. Then, in his loneliness, he got into the habit of speaking to it as he had been told to do. Sometimes he spoke in exasperation. He had no patience when it answered him in a screechy mimicry of what he said, and he often lost his temper with it.

He was sitting drinking in the small hours, still trying to arrange the poems in his anthology and decide what to keep in and what to leave out, when the bird suddenly spoke to him. He couldn't make out the words, and he turned on it peevishly. "Shut up you yellow basket!"

Riki fluttered to the top of his ladder, flounced there in a bad temper, and gave back the insult. "Ya yella basket."

He came down again, still flapping. He made angry little noises, and his chest went out in defiance. He looked fierce. With his beak through the cage he threatened clearly.

"I'll tell Nan."

Mr Green rose, shaking his fist, his voice raised.

"You'll tell Nan? I'm the one that'll tell Nan! I'll tell her what you are - you're a little pest!"

The moment the words were out of his mouth, he was shocked at himself.

"What the hell am I doing? Arguing with a brainless bird! What a stupid thing to say - 'I'm the one that'll tell Nan.'"

He didn't get the chance to tell Nan anything. His visits to the hospital were an ordeal. Soon they were pointless. She lay in a trance, grey and mute. The death certificate said she died of a cerebral tumour.

He was less fit for living alone than he thought he would be. He began to drink more every night, starting earlier and finishing later. Even so, his sleep was broken. He went to the doctor and asked for sleeping pills.

His days were heavy with grief, and the unwanted legacy of Riki was only a nuisance. But he still hadn't the heart to sell or destroy the bird. He knew Nan wouldn't like it, and although she was gone for ever he had a persistent feeling, a faith or a hope, that she lived on somewhere and saw all he did, and knew even his most secret thoughts. So whenever the bird was silent for a long spell he spoke to it gently for her sake. Sometimes, when it spoke without his encouragement, he felt it was really talking to Nan in a private dialogue, where all he was allowed to hear was what the bird said. He was frightened by the thought of a pet bird conversing with a dead woman.

He broke down completely one midnight in December. To comfort his loneliness he often spoke aloud, and now he chatted to Nan as if she were still there. He asked her to come and talk to Riki. He raised his voice. He knew he had to shout to make her hear, she was so far away. And he badly wanted her help, for he had no conversation for a bird, or for anybody.

The loud voice excited Riki. He screeched his own appeals, and in spasms of chatter he repeated all the phrases Nan had ever taught him. He stopped as abruptly as he had started, and peered through his cage.

The sad look in the little eyes made Mr Green remember he hadn't opened the cage for a couple of days. He apologised to the pining bird, and released it. He watched it fly across the room in short flights, perching here and there for a moment. Then it soared to the top of the bureau-bookcase, and settled there on a bust of Milton Mr Green had bought in a junk shop years ago. From that height it looked curiously down on the drunk man.

A sudden rustling in the curtains startled Mr Green. But it was only the wind coming through a window not properly closed. That, and nothing more. He turned and stared at the silent bird. Its beak went on tapping gently on the shoulder of the bust. Mr Green screamed.

"Stop that!"

The bird glared, grim and ominous.

Mr Green raised an accusing finger and staggered as he ranted.

"I know who you are! I cut you out of my anthology! 'The fowl whose fiery eyes' . . . 'Once upon a midnight dreary . . .'"

Riki didn't answer, and Mr Green lurched away. He poured another whisky, and before he put the bottle down he held it up to the light. There wasn't much left. He pondered, weak and weary, then decided.

"I've had a lot tonight. I'll take no more."

Riki echoed him, lamenting.

"No more Nan. Bed Nan. No more."

Mr Green looked up at the bird again. He remembered the night he had seen Nan feed it with moistened crumbs, and then wipe its beak. He spoke to it viciously.

"Dirty face! That's what Nan called you. And you know what I called you? A little pest - you're a little pest."

He swayed, clicked his fingers at the bird, and whispered kindly.

"You miss Nan? She was my pal. I miss Nan."

Stately on Milton's head Riki counter-claimed.

"My pal."

Mr Green knew his grief would never end so long as this unreasonable creature went on evoking the woman who was gone. He waved his hands at the bookcase, trying to get the bird to come down.

"Come on now! Back into your cage. I'll tell you what I'll do."

Riki obeyed him in its own good time.

Mr Green started again.

"I'll tell you what. We'll both go and see Nan. You can tell Nan and I'll tell Nan. What do you think of that? Only, you go first."

He moved with care to carry out his plan. He crumbled three sleeping pills on a dessert spoon and damped them with a generous drop of whisky. Through the door of the cage he offered the mixture.

Riki took it with grave and stern decorum. He sagged when the spoon was empty, gawked, and dropped to the floor.

Mr Green went upstairs to the bathroom, put into a glass of water all the pills he had left and gulped them down. Then he drank the rest of his whisky, went into the bedroom and lay down in the dark.

George Friel

With acknowledgements to the George Friel archive in the National Library of Scotland. A Friend of Humanity, Friel's collected stories edited by Gordon Jarvie, will appear next year from Polygon. This story was submitted to the BBC in 1974 but never broadcast.

Translations by David Purves

from the Chinese of Po Chu-I (772-846)

AULD AGE

We are growein auld thegither, you an me;
we maun ask oursells, 'whatlyke is eild?'
The bleirie ee is steik't or nicht faws;
the fekless heid is aye unkaimed at nuin.
Stelled bi a staff, whyles a wee turn outby;
or aw day sittin wi steikit doors.
A daurna glisk i the keikin gless;
A canna read smaw-prentit buiks.
Deeper an deeper A loue the auld freins;
thir days A've littil troke wi yungir men.
But yae thing juist: the pleisure o idle blether,
is gleg as evir, whan you an A forgether.

WUNTER NICHT

Ma houss is puir an thaim A loue haes left me.
Ma corp is seik - A canna jyne the feast.
The'r no leevin sowl forenent ma een
as A ligg ma lane lock't in ma cot-houss chaumer.
Ma brukken cruisie burns wi a dwaiblie lowe.
Ma tattert drapes hing squint an dinna meet.
'Fuff' on the front dure-step an wundae sill,
again an again A hear the new snaw faw.
Day in, day oot, the aulder A growe A sleep the less.
A wauken the midnicht oor an sit up strecht in bed.
Gin a haedna lairnt the airt o meditation,
hou could A beir this yondmaist laneliness?
Steive an sterk ma bodie hauds the yird;
unhinnert nou ma sowl devauls ti entropie.
Sae haes it been for fower dreich year:
a thousan an thrie hunder nicht!

LOSSIN A SLAVE-QUYNE

Aroun ma howf the littil waw is laich.
At the wynd door hir loss wes leitit late.
A'm shamed ti think that whyles we warna kynd;
A'm vext anent yeir tyauvin that wul nevir
be repeyed. The cagit burd is no behauden.
The wund-thrawn flouers clauchtsna the tree.

Whaur the-nicht she liggs the'r nane can gie us wurd;
Naebody kens, but the bricht owre-watchin muin.

REVIEWS

THE ENLIGHTENMENT REVIEWED

The Tradition of Scottish Philosophy: A New Perspective on the Enlightenment, Alexander Broadie, Polygon £7.95

Alexander Broadie has produced a brilliant and invaluable book which draws coherently together the main lines of logical, philosophical and moral thought in two creative periods of Scottish philosophy, from pre-Reformation schoolmen and churchmen to the great thinkers of the Scottish Enlightenment, Hutcheson, Hume, Reid and Adam Smith. The book rescues from long neglect the far-reaching achievements John Mair and his circle at the universities of Paris and St Andrews. Dr Broadie has thrown a flood of light not only upon the intellectual contribution of people like John Ireland, George Lokert or William Manderston, as well as Mair, but has brought to light a coherent intellectual tradition in the history of Scottish philosophy. As such it deserves a significant place along with the work of George Davie in *The Democratic Intellect*, and Richard Olson in *Scottish Philosophy and British Physics 1750-1880*.

Dr Broadie's emphasis upon the constructive contribution of Scottish thinkers in the decades around 1500 is not intended to belittle the contribution of later men of the Scottish Enlightenment, but to correct a seriously distorted picture of the history of Scottish culture and philosophy in particular. In highly schematic fashion he sketches the lines of thought between pre-Reformation figures like Laurence of Lindores through Reformation figures like Andrew Melville and Robert Rollock, to the renewed attention given after the Reformation to the linguistic and conceptual problems of nominalism and realism that cropped up with such force after the rise of Newtonian physics, and thus to questions about existence, the external world, free will, that still beset present-day philosophers.

The second chapter is devoted to "philosophy in the Scots Tongue" as presented in *The Mirror of Wisdom* by John Ireland (completed 1490) in the nominalist tradition of Lawrence of Lindores at St Andrews. Emphasis is laid upon the freedom of God in creating the world and in His acts towards it relating to His transcendent will; but also upon the freedom of man to obey or disobey God's law. Of particular interest is the point raised by Ireland of the erroneous way in which human beings speak of God through their tendency to think of him in causal and temporal terms. Dr Broadie not only reveals important similarities between the two great periods in the development of Scottish philosophy in the 16th and 18th centuries, but draws out a deeply significant co-ordination between them in respect of their epistemological approaches. "The Circle of John Mair" was centred in the College of Montaigu in Paris (where Erasmus, George Buchanan, John Calvin and Ignatius Loyola had also studied at various times). In addition to Mair himself, an account is offered of its leading members, David Cranston, George Lokert, William Manderston, Robert Galbraith, James Liddell, Gilbert Crab and Hector Boece. Broadie considers the positions adopted in their theory of knowledge, in which a movement of thought takes place between a critical nominalism and realism, not unlike that movement of thought between Hume and Reid. Attention is given to the relation between language and notions of the building blocks of mental language, whether a natural or conventional relation obtains between them, and thus to a contrast between a nominalist and a realist theory of meaning.

On the one hand, Dr Broadie shows that for John Mair notions or mental terms are acts of the understanding (*actus intelligendi*). That might be understood in a nominalist way which places the weight upon the act of the mind itself rather than upon the reality intended. Mair rejected the conception of images in the middle, the idea that the act of understanding terminates upon an image or representation of some reality and not immediately upon the reality itself. Hence if the mind entertains images or representations, as it must, the understanding acts *through* them, not by means of them. It would appear that John Mair works in the last resort with a realist rather than a nominalist theory of signification and knowledge. This is the way in which one must understand John Mair, if one interprets him in the light of his great hero, John Duns Scotus, whose Paris lectures on the *Sentences* of Peter Lombard Mair edited and published as *Reportata Parisiensa* (now known as *Lectura*).

While Mair certainly made use of nominalist, and terminist, tools, he did so to establish a realist position which he inherited from Duns Scotus, evident in his deployment of the Scotist distinction between primary and secondary intentions. Dr Broadie, unfortunately, leaves Duns Scotus out of his account (although he speaks of him as "the first truly great Scottish philosopher"), on the ground that Scotus had not taught in Scotland and had flourished two centuries earlier. It is ultimately the critical realism of Duns Scotus, not least in its bearing upon John Mair himself, that Dr Broadie brilliantly establishes in the tradition of Scottish philosophy.

Broadie then turns to the issue of evident and

inevident assent. Evident assent is caused by principles which necessitate the intellect, i.e. through either the direct causality of the object or through necessary logical connections. The theological implications of this are awesome, in face of the kind of assent that not even God can do anything to prevent in securing its effect! Mair also discusses two kinds of inevident assent. One is opinion, and the other is faith. In the latter case, while assent involves an act of will, it is not assent without reason - e.g. through trust in some person or religious authority, or on the grounds of probability. Thus philosophers hold that unless there is evidence for a given proposition we cannot have faith in it. The argument carries the reader into the perennial question of free will and grace, with restricted reference to the teaching of William Manderston. The issue at stake here is that between a voluntarist and a realist conception of grace and of belief. This was the great issue between Pelagian and Augustinian approaches raised by Gregory of Rimini towards the end of the Middle Ages, but a burning issue at the Reformation. The interest here, however, lies in Manderston's criticism of the view of Robert Holkot that every act of believing is purely natural and is caused by purely natural motives which necessitate the understanding. Manderston argues, instead, for a conception of belief in which a significant place is and must be given to the human will which, according to Dr Broadie, may help us see more clearly how we should respond to Hume's discussion of the same topic. While not Pelagian, it is one in which full weight of responsibility is laid upon our free will.

Dr Broadie then turns to "The Post-Mediaeval Period" in the tradition of Scottish philosophy, concentrating on the transition in logic and linguistic style during the Renaissance. Particular attention is given to the different use of Aristotle in the thought of people like William Cranston of St Andrews and Robert Rollock of Edinburgh, and to their view of logic as subsidiary to the art of rhetoric. Dr Broadie traces here the impact of Rudolph Agricola the Dutch (not Italian!) humanist in his book De Inventione Dialectica, but he seems to miss the real point of the transition which began with the epoch-making work of Lorenzo Valla, In dialecticen, to which Agricola was heavily indebted. This was an attempt to move away from the abstract questions raised by the mediaeval schoolmen to which only logical answers could be given, to the development of genuine scientific questions about realities that yield positive answers. The model taken by Valla was from Cicero's account of the way in which evidence is subjected to open interrogative questioning in a court of law in order to bring the truth to light on its own evidential grounds. This was the procedure that led to the exposure of "the False Decretals", that was to influence John Calvin, was built into Renaissance law, and then had a powerful impact on Francis Bacon and the rise of empirical scientific inquiry - that is, the very procedure that was later taken up during the Scottish Enlightenment and led to the epoch-making discoveries of James Clerk Maxwell.

Broadie seems to think that "logic was a casualty of the Reformation"! That judgment applies rather to Peter Ramus, who attempted to formulate a logical method of scientific discovery through a bowdlerisation of Aristotle's Posterior Analytics, which had a damaging effect on Scottish universities through Melville and Rollock. Due to his aversion to Ramist logic Samuel Rutherford reverted to an older approach to Aristotle that Broadie notices. The lesson the reformers learned, however, was that, while logic has its proper place in clarifying interrelations among ideas and statements, it has no place in determining the relation of ideas to being, or of statements to empirical reality. The rational is deeper and wider than the logical, and can apply to relations between empirical realities or events as the logical does not. Thus they opened up the road for a new appreciation of history which was to have a decided effect on the Scottish Enlightenment. Attention to history was also influenced by the study of Jewish writings and the study of Hebrew to which Broadie alludes several times.

Dr Broadie points out that Robert Balfour, a pupil of Samuel Rutherford, quotes Philo Judaeus (as well as Agricola, Valla and Ramus!) among his sources. That was typical of the reformed tradition in theology as we can see, for example, in the great Syntagma Theologiae of Polanus, long used as a regular textbook in theology by Scottish Presbyteries, and clearly well known to David Hume. This is evident in the fact that Hume borrowed the distinction between archetypal and ectypal analogy which Polanus cited from Philo, and put it into the mouth of "Philo" the interlocutor in his Dialogues on Natural Religion, who obviously best represents Hume's own mind. In that work of Polanus regular attention was devoted to the views of Duns Scotus set over against those of Thomas Aquinas, another indication of the continuing impact of Scotist thought upon the Scottish tradition of in theology and philosophy.

These suggestions do not detract from Dr Broadie's purpose and work, but reinforce his penetrating insights in tracing a line of influence from Mair's circle to the philosophers of the Scottish Enlightenment. In particular I believe that to establish the scientific method of investigating nature that was indebted to Valla, with which Mair himself was acquainted, establishes even more firmly the transition from sixteenth century thought to the science of human nature in the eighteenth century. I find it exciting to be shown by Dr Broadie that the transition from a nominalist empiricism to a critical realism found in post-mediaeval thought has a parallel in the way in which Scottish philosophy moved under the influence of Francis Hutcheson and Adam Smith through the nominalist empiricism of David Hume to the critical realism of the Common Sense approach to knowledge of the external world attempted by Thomas Reid. Here Broadie argues that "the role of notions in Mair's thought is the same as ideas in Reid's. (1) Just as Mair regards notions as operations of the mind, so does Reid regard ideas. (2) Just as Mair leaves no room for an object of knowledge intermediate between the notion of X and the external object X, so also Reid leaves no room for an object of knowledge intermediate between an idea, considered as a mental operation, and the object of which the idea is an idea ... Thus (3) just as Mair is not at all skeptical about the existence of external objects, neither is Reid."

Broadie points out that Hume's position, that the occurrence of belief is explained by natural necessity and not by will, is essentially the same as Robert Holkot, but in that even the criticism of Holkot's concept of belief made by Manderston is equally effective against Hume. Broadie shows that the philosophical dispute in the mid eighteenth had been anticipated early in the sixteenth century, and that underlying the dispute about belief and will there is a conflict between two radically different concepts of man. Far from Manderston's position being dismissed it represents a serious challenge to the science of man Hume sought to construct.

In his concluding chapter, Dr Broadie takes account of the difference made to the philosophical scenario in Scotland by the Cartesian revolution in philosophy and the advent of Newtonian mechanics. Nevertheless, the thesis holds good, that in respect of philosophy the Pre-Reformation period matches the Enlightenment, and that a basic line of continuity in the tradition of Scottish Philosophy can be traced from one to the other. This is one of the most interesting and perceptive books on the history of Scottish thought I have ever read. It provides a new perspective on the Enlightenment, restores intellectual balance in the appreciation of our culture, and opens up the field in a fresh and exciting way for further research. Dr Broadie has put us immensely in his debt.

Thomas F. Torrance

RAPE AND THE ACT OF UNION

Alasdair Gray, *Something Leather*, Jonathan Cape, £12.95; *McGrotty and Ludmilla*, Dog and Bone, £5.00.

My reading tends to be governed by chance rather than intent, and an unusually sustained run of poverty had meant that I did not read anything of Alasdair Gray's after *1982, Janine*, so it was with some anticipation that I opened *Something Leather*. I had noted how fond reviewers were of declaring his later books "not as good as *Lanark*". As most of the books I had read in the interim were also not as good as *Lanark*, I was keen to find out how substandard Gray compared with supposedly top-notch William Lloyd, A N Wilson, Ian McEwan and so on.

The first interesting thing I discovered was that he didn't really compare at all. This supported the reviewers, who never once mentioned Amis *père* or *fils* in Gray's vicinity, though they used these French words so frequently elsewhere as to make me wonder if that Aged Curmudgeon had shifted policy on the European question.

Gray could have been compared instead to James Kelman, from whom he borrows the neat technique of representing English middle-class speech phonetically. He could have been compared with Kathy Acker, from whom he took the suggestion of basing the book around the sexual awakening of a female rather than his usual male. But in all the reviews I read he was obstinately compared to himself. The effect of this was to turn the book into a kind of bottled specimen, "The Scottish Novel, *circa* 1990". I was reminded of Superman, who keeps a miniaturised city in a bottle in his Ice Fortress at the North Pole, and doesn't show it to anyone.

So what was different? Articulating simply, I would say that Alasdair Gray tells the truth. If he doesn't have much of an idea for a book and has to throw in some plays and short stories to pad it out, he tells us. Basically *Something Leather* is about a woman who is forcibly seduced by a trio of lesbians. This story occurs in Chapter One and Twelve. Between these two points Gray uses his "other" material to suggest why it happens. Then at the end he describes this process, giving a section from an earlier draft. Reviewers (I'm not going to tell you who they are!) used this as grounds for dismissing the whole as trumped-up sexual fantasy. For some reason, this did not remind them of *London Fields*.

Gray draws characters possessed of a singular and attractive combination of energy and self-awareness. I don't mean the ones we are meant to find sexually attractive, but people like Tom Lang, the blustering Scottish businessman, whose relish

for his brief trajectory of success is almost poignant. Or the headmistress of an exclusive if not top-notch girls' school whose hermetic philosophy is nearly convincing, as here where she teaches masturbation and social theory:

> Everybody, Harriet, has ideas which make them tingle, ideas which make stroking themselves and even stroking otha people moa fun. These ideas a to be found in litritcha, art, films, advertisements and the games we play. Some of these ideas would be harmful if taken seriously, but only stupid people take ideas seriously . . . in England we are all liberals at heart, as wise as serpents and harmless as doves. We know that the wildest ideas are just ways of adding funny tingly feelings to a world managed by old fashioned business methods, methods no serious person questions.

Harriet, the abused child from a privileged background, is the novel's most interesting creation. She miraculously sprang into existence when Gray tried to stick his story together, becoming its necessary cement. A sado-masochist who sculpts instead of speaking, her improbable development is lovingly described via her all-too-probable creations, up to the projected positioning of her largest installation, the Bum Garden, firmly on the face of Glasgow, City of Culture. Harry, as she is known (except on pp 23, 145 and 151, where, for reasons I cannot help you with, she is called 'Judy'), forms an English principle, which is set against June Tain, the book's cover star and victim of the lesbian assault. June is Scottish. Two working-class women, Donalda and Senga (no, I don't know any working-class women called by these names either), conspire with Harry in the assault. My dim sense of June as a Scottish muse and the rape as the Act of Union allows me to declare the book to be symbolically satisfying, but this isn't the main reason I enjoy it.

Gray's candour, and the sense this gives of the mysteriousness of the creative process, inclines me towards defining a quality of Scottish prose, and perhaps poetry. By removing some of the illusions of elitism which surround the writing process (though 'honesty' is arguably a further illusion), writers like Gray, Kelman, W S Graham and MacDiarmid suggest something those critics mentioned earlier find hard to swallow. This bitter pill being: perhaps literature is accessible, perhaps all you have to do is sit down and read it with a (very) open mind.

I can think of many people for whom this suggestion is not a truism, for whom literature is something as threatening as it is ridiculous. Gray's book, in which the skeleton is plainly visible, seems to me to escape the charge of irrelevance such people bring against books. Those novelists I mentioned at the start of this review seem to me to do the opposite, to exacerbate by their professional veneer a sense that literature exists as a fashion accessory to a particular class.

Large claims. So large that I have no room to discuss *McGrotty and Ludmilla*, except to say that, as someone who finds English politics deeply boring, I found the book amusing enough, though not as amusing as the idea that Scots are actually involved in the parliamentary 'process' at a meaningful level. The idea of putting a comment at the top of each page was completely lost on me until page 63, and even then I forgot about it soon after, unlike the typographic error on pp 131-132 of *Something Leather*, which continues to force itself on my consciousness at odd intervals.

W N Herbert

THE WELL-DRESSED EMPEROR

Kenneth White: *Travels in the Drifting Dawn*, Penguin, £4.99; *The Blue Road*, £12.95; *Handbook for the Diamond Country*, both Mainstream, £12.95; *The Bird Path*, Penguin, £5.99.

So much hype surrounds Kenneth White that it is hard to see his writing as it is. He has attained in France, says the blurb to *The Bird Path*, "the status of an intellectual culture hero who points the way beyond the exhausted discourses of the late twentieth century." I am reminded of a number of French "culture heroes", such as Jean-Luc Godard and Michel Foucault, whose reputations were cracked up with so much intellectual pretension that one scarcely dared to perceive one's honest reaction. Not that, in the case of White, the Emperor has no clothes. On the contrary, he is excellently dressed, though not in the absurd space-age gear suggested by the phrase 'culture hero'.

Two of the books are accounts of travels. *Travels in the Drifting Dawn* is an attractive miscellany of wanderings in Scotland, Ireland, Belgium, Brittany etc. *The Blue Road* is a more ambitious account of a trip to Labrador, seen in metaphysical terms: "Labrador is where I come full circle, swallow my birth, develop all the negatives of my adolescence and get a good look at my original face. What I need above all at the moment is space, a big white breathing space for the ultimate meditation." Written diary-style in short, clearly-seen passages, most a few paragraphs long, it is a vivid account of the journey. The simplicity of the writing accommodates a great many learned references, often to early explorers, geologists, and Buddhist writers. In a poem at the end he writes a sort of credo: "a man needs to fix his knowledge/ but he also needs an emptiness/ in which to move". *Handbook for the*

Diamond Country is a collected shorter poems; The Bird Path a collected longer. The short poems have a Buddhist simplicity, sometimes very beautiful ('Rosy Quartz', 'The Wandering Jew'), sometimes a bit sparse: "OK/ have another sip of honeyed wine/ and let's move on".

He loves open space, vistas, snow, mountains. "This is the summit of contemplation, and/ no art can touch it/ blue, so blue, the far-out archipel-ago/ and the sea shimmering, shimmering" ('A High Blue Day on Scalpay'). He also loves the colour white. Earlier poems, more varied, contain some darkness, and I confess I find it a relief.

In The Bird Path (longer poems and stories) we meet what is in my opinion the most impressive work. The three sections at the end, originally a collection called Atlantica, are lovely and profound, and give White room to develop his thought and escape the flavour of the "egotistical sublime" which can be annoying in some short poems and in The Blue Road. His account of a birch wood ('Valley of Birches'), of whalers ('The Western Gateways'), or of 'Brandan's Last Voyage' gives one a beautiful sense of a genuinely meditative and empathic mind.

One word used of White by several admirers is "unclassifiable". This is based on a confusion. White's impulse in his writing is mystical (though he claims there is "nothing religious about him"), to experience the world afresh, in all the mystery of its unique and differentiated being, freed from the banality of classification. But to seek to go beyond classification is not to be unclassifiable, and White belongs clearly in a tradition, mainly American, which includes writers like Emerson, Whitman, Henry Miller and Gary Snyder.

These people, like White, have been influenced by Eastern mystical ideas, especially Buddhist and Taoist, without ceasing to belong in the western world or be aware of science and the problems of modern life. All, in different ways, tend to repudiate much of mainstream Euro-American literature; they wish to live with both sensual and intellectual intensity; they wish to report how it is to be alive for a short time and in particular places in an astonishing and marvellous universe. They tend rather to bypass the complexities of psychological and social life, and this is their limitation, as it is the limitation of traditional Buddhism. They tend therefore to seem alien in complicated social Europe. The great novel, opera, the paintings of Rubens are not their scene. But many European writers, including Hugh MacDiarmid, and also such French poets as Michaux and Guillevic, may also be linked with them. White is not "unclassifiable": he belongs, at his best very impressively, in a great modern tradition.

D M Black

FABER POETRY

Andrew Motion, Love in a Life; Philip Gross, The Son of the Duke of Nowhere; Oliver Reynolds, The Oslo Tram; Christopher Logue, Kings, Faber & Faber paperback, £4.99.

"Best of all is my voice from the springing south:/ brilliant, particular leaves come rioting out of my mouth." This declarative note of cultural allegiance at the end of Andrew Motion's 'Cleaned Out' reflects the wider assuredness of his publisher, launching under new editorship a poetry list for the new decade proclaimed as a continuation of "The Great Tradition" of Eliot, Auden, Larkin, Hughes et al. Precisely what is intended by 'Great Tradition' - Faber's record as the publisher synonymous with the major, multinational poetic achievements of Modernism and beyond, or the High Church of an 'English' poetic mainstream - remains conveniently ambiguous.

Motion's moment of assertion is short-lived in a volume which, hinting at an ultimately elusive overall narrative coherence, explores the anxieties of identity caught in a matrix of conflicting pressures, historical, personal and political. His stylistic antecedents, Edward Thomas and Philip Larkin, stalk these pages and literally inhabit them as ghosts: Browning is an added spectre, from whom the book's title is taken. Hauntings, in fact, abound. The persona of Part One is either haunted by powerful subconscious images, like the hallucinatory nightmare of a Victorian man aboard a train bearing a withered lily in a jar (Browning?) in 'Bad Dreams', or is himself haunting those around him following 'deaths' metaphorical and imaginary, as in 'Close':

Nobody spoke about me
or how I was no longer there.
It was odd, but I understood why:
when I had drowned I was only
a matter of yards out to sea
(not too far out - too close),
still able to hear the talk
and have everything safe in view.

The paradox of selfhood, threatened by the fear that "time would run out/ and you'd see yourself dead" - underlines a mood of oppressive morbidity, trapping both speaker and idiom in a "dream that time/ will last long enough/ to let me die happy" ('Look'). A sensuously registered thirst and the taste of water serve as a reminder that "I am dying at home" ('Judgement'); a painful memory of childhood pitches the adult into a sea of anonymity and the sensation of being "dead to the world" ('Cutting'), a sensation half-desired and half-dreaded. Occasionally the neurosis is numbed by shots of cynicism, as in 'The Vision of that Ancient Man', declaring "I know I wanted to die", concluding "Sod it; who cares?" By this stage it's difficult not to agree.

Motion deploys random images of suffering, drowning, and dramatic fatal accidents which eventually fall into pattern, juxtaposed with themes of domestic innocence besieged by alien forces. A wife giving birth to twins is metamorphosed horribly into the speaker's mother dying of cancer on a hospital bed in 'Look'. In 'One Who Disappeared' a bathetic anecdote about a man blown from a clifftop by a violent gust of wind becomes a chilling metaphor for a small child, buffeted helplessly by the throes of illness. Motion's celebrated facility with direct narrative address is ideally suited to such strategies, but only in Parts Two and Three where he breaks free of this cloying introspection to confront wider issues - suppression in Prague, a nightmarish and enigmatic search in Belfast - does the verse becomes in any way memorable. 'Bone Elephant', perhaps the finest moment of the book, fuses Motion's themes by counterpointing a father's memories of the Second World War with the recent traumas of East European revolution, the poem unified around the symbol of crushing tanks and the apparently trivial ornament of the title.

As the title of his fifth collection indicates, Philip Gross's poetry is forced out from strenuous political realities which Motion can only flirt with as a spectator. A mind captive to the displacement and dispossession of his exiled Estonian background, forms not only the recurrent motif of these poems but also an urgent creative dynamic. How the mind can deal with 'anywhere' if your imaginative home is 'nowhere' forms the terrible, imponderable polarity explored in the title poem with its intense, imagistic focus: "Here, me,/ watching. There, trains, going away." The fragility of memory emerges as the collection's most insistent theme, the striving for 'the one fixed point' on ever-fluctuating borders: the boy waiting by the shore for the tide to recede and expose the carcass of a shipwreck in 'The Ark'. In 'Saying When', speculation on the moment of the death of a loved one becomes not merely a metaphor for loss of collective history, but a wider emblem of the act of creative cognition itself - 'no sooner seen than gone'. It's testimony to Gross's versatility in form and diction that this theme of displacement is by no means confined to the wistful or nostalgic, but can be imparted through poignant humour - exile envisaged as a radio you can't tune properly as in 'Lahti' - or stringent satire in the tradition of European peripheries' cynical defiance of oppression:

Out in the woods, the ants are building empires,

ziggurats of dead wood, towers of Babel.
They need only a flagpole; I plant my stick.
Hundreds swarm up: At the top, they wave
then blunder back, wagging antennae: *Brothers,*

turn back! There has been some mistake . .
('A Summit in Slovenia')

In contrast to the claustrophobic flatness of Motion's idiom, the brightness in the register of these poems is rarely dulled despite Gross's willingness to take risks in contrasting structures and textures, ranging from the fragmentary to the discursive extended narrative straying into poetic prose. Gross has an equal ingenuity in exloiting disparities of perspective, particularly in those pieces on landscape: in 'The End of the Line', an older woman and a young girl grudgingly share either side of a train compartment on a futile journey as "Their windows run different channels"; in the oddly MacCaig-like 'What the Mountain Saw', mountain observes man as much as the other way round. "If one could stand there/ looking down . . . this would all be very small," the man concludes, the preceding eleven stanzas having already dramatised the profundity of his speculation. The last four pieces extend a concern with human frailty through different metaphorical devices - a crumbling house, invisibly decaying human skin, a fairground big wheel, children's rhymes - with a note of resigned gravity unusual for a poet still not quite forty. In every other sense, this is a poetry of distinctive vigour and vitality from a talent worth watching.

Though his relationship with the place is correspondingly obtuse, the Norway and Oslo backdrop to much of Oliver Reynolds' work imparts a rejuvinating vividness to language and theme suggestive of Gross's Estonia, though Reynolds' responsiveness to eclectic subject-matter is if anything more pronounced. Likewise in technique and design. From the title poem:

Year by year
this old woman
next to the ticket punch
is translating Dostoevsky
Night by night
she sleeps
in an iron lung
the wreck of her chest
grinding uphill
Returning from the library
she now sways
in the sunlit lung
of the tram

The first dozen poems offer an intriguing mirror-image of the conventional typography of the remaining eighteen by justifying the right and leaving the left margin ragged, accentuating a form in which poems 'happen' line by fragmented line in a process of jerky, associative randomness. The peculiar tug to the eye combined with the terse bumpiness in sense makes this verse vividly experiential in an oddly physical way, to compelling effect in longer narratives such as 'From the Second Hell', a stark enactment of the burning of a mediaeval poet for heresy, and 'Synopticon', a hypnotic theological discourse on the origins of St Mark's testament offset by allusions to more contemporary martyrs like Victor Jara.

The "twists and turns" in the "denuded style" of the journalist in 'O', another lengthy piece, might be taken as self-referential, and the effect would be wearying were it not for the fluency Reynolds exhibits in the conventional remainder of the collection, where blank verse and stanzaic formulae take over. There is occasional obliquity and prolixity here, a tendency to discursive aimlessness where the strictures of the experimental technique are conspicuously absent. When Reynolds *does* rein himself in, however, by alighting on a subject demanding technical and thematic constraint, the effects can be startling, especially in the fleeting portrait: 'Professor' opens incisively with "She has a sixth finger/ she fills from a bottle", and closes in wonderfully grotesque simile: "Behind thick spectacles,/ book-dimmed eyes flit at you/ like fish butting their tanks." Often energised by social and urban themes, maybe Reynolds' true direction lies in this sharp, satirical observation which can explode into the extraordinarily evocative and felicitous image. One such moment in 'Oliver and Tone Have Moved to Chelsea', a refreshing swipe at London yuppies, is worth the whole volume:

High above the city, a plane draws out
a slow burr of sound like a glass-cutter
scoring a window. One tap and you're through.

Space permits only brief reference to Christopher Logue's *Kings*, the latest instalment of an idiosyncratic account of Homer's *Iliad* based on a 'translation' in its loosest sense - really a process of imaginative re-creation. Possibly too loose: Logue is so eager to utilise a large armament of techniques, registers and perspectives that the methodology often overshadows the result, as if the project has become fraught with the weight of its own endeavour. Perhaps future instalments will serve to clarify its purpose.

Interesting indications, then, of the future development of Faber's 'Great Tradition', depending on whose or which tradition you mean. Is contemporary English poetry 'cleaned out' or 'riotously springing'? A bit of both.

Gavin Wallace

MIXED DOUBLES

The Double in 19th Century Fiction, John Herdman, Macmillan, £35; *A Concussed History of Scotland, A Novel of Another Sort*, Frank Kuppner, Polygon, £7.95; Alan Bold, *An Open Book*, Macdonald (Lines Review Eds), £8.95.

John Herdman makes the theological background of the double in literature abundantly clear, and the highlights of his study include Germany (for the provision of the Doppelganger) and Scotland, home of Dr Jekyll as well as Mr Hyde. A better pre-19th century example even than Marlowe's *Faustus* would have been Jacob Bidermann's *Cenodoxus* of 1600, of which the Edinburgh Bilingual Library produced a fine translation in 1975 by D G Dyer and Cecily Longrigg. The Romantics are the central matter of the book, however, though the term "nineteenth century" might have been stretched a bit to afford a glance at the equally disturbing *Der blonde Eckbert* of Tieck. Dr Herdman concentrates in his concise and readable book on E T A Hoffmann and *The Devil's Elixirs*, moving from that to Hogg's *Justified Sinner*, and from there to Poe (not Mark Twain where there might have been possibilities), and on to Gogol and Dostoyevsky before concluding the century with Stevenson and his awareness of the "sharply over-defined opposition between good and evil," and finally Maupassant and Wilde. We begin with theology and end with psychology, its *alter ego*, with the century of Freud, and more especially Jung, and one might wish that the work could have embraced also that historically misplaced writer Stefan Zweig and *The Royal Game*, where the German dualism shown up in Celan's *Todesfuge* drives a representative of an older Europe to become his own double over the chessboard. Political doubling, of course, was provided after the Second World War in the rejoined twin Germanies, but that is beyond the scope of Dr Herdman's fascinating book.

The fly-leaf blurb for Frank Kuppner's latest novel explains that the work defies reductive characterisation and neat pigeonholing, taking this to be an advantage. Certainly it defies brief description, and the blurb at the back of the work calls it "A Concise History . . . Another Sort of Novel" in mirror-writing, it does indeed challenge the barriers between disciplines. A review of previous novels used the word "allsorts", but the problem with the experimental novel is not the novelty, nor even the distant and reproachful tone of E M Forster, but whether the emperor really has any clothes on? In this case, he is probably naked, but with pieces of good jewellery.

Kuppner is not without literary ancestors, even

if *Tristram Shandy* is more coherent, *Finnegans Wake* has better words (though the Polish-German name *Ogurkenschnecke* - "cucumber-snail" - has nice Freudian resonances), *The Story of the Eye* more brutal pornography, and Wittgenstein's notebooks more substance. "History is a surface so complicated that it looks like infinite depth," but the whole is less a history of anywhere than another illustration of the Scottish penchant for the double. The novel is a dialogue between the author and his double, the reader. The clue is in Chapter 422: "if this is not you, then no doubt it is someone else - though I strongly suspect that it is you. After all, you are a known liar and hypocrite, aren't you?" *Hypocrite lecteur, mon semblable, mon frère*. Summary is impossible for the surreal-epigrammatic, though there are good lines, with the speculation that a cell from J S Bach linked with a cell from Shakespeare would produce a "highly intelligent builder's labourer with a never-discovered gift for dancing." But the choices include literary self-indulgence, self-conscious masturbation before a hypocrite audience, or holding up a broken mirror where there are plenty of whole ones about. The trouble with taking us into a "territory where very little is fixed" (fly-leaf again) is that questions of value tend to come unstuck.

Alan Bold's reprinted essays have the title *An Open Book* (a nice title-page joke, in fact), to assert his "belief in the accessibility of art." The clear and far-reaching introduction to *The Martial Muse* is there, though away from its context one wishes the essay were longer, and developed some of the adumbrated points: is good pro-war poetry possible? The inclusion of the "We shall fight them on the beaches" speech as poetry is admirable, but one wonders about the *"Hassgesang gegen England"*. 'Scotlit' is another welcome inclusion, and it picks up the Scottish good-and-evil dualism that welcomed the double in literature. The parading of national archetypes, however, is always a little nationalistic, and perhaps everyone is proud of his archetypes (Harry Lauder's Scotchness is a parallel to George Formby's Lancastrianism, also exported from its native soil). Television (latterly via John Byrne) continues to reaffirm them. The other essays are on 'Poetry and Socialism' (now with an increasingly historical feel), on 'Bellany and Scottish Painting', and on writers as diverse as John le Carré, Auden and MacDiarmid, but also Tolkien as a poet, in which context Bold provides a welcome appreciation of the revival of alliterative verse in "The Homecoming of Beorhtnoth"; the link with the *Battle of Maldon* takes us back to the study of war poetry. The final essay, written for the *Glasgow Herald*, discusses a variety of

recent poetic and other biographies. It is pushed a little out of focus now, perhaps, by Anne Stevenson's biography of Sylvia Plath, and also, as a minor pendant to Hillier on Betjeman, by Humphrey Carpenter on C S Lewis. But it is appropriate as a final piece because it ends with comments from the workroom, on the genesis of Bold's own biography of MacDiarmid.

Brian Murdoch

THEATRICAL BOOKS

Scotfree: New Scottish Plays, A Cameron (ed), Nick Hern Books, £7.95; *The Bone Won't Break*, John McGrath, £7.99; *The Moon Belongs to Everyone*, Elizabeth MacLennan, £9.99, Methuen.

A decade of Thatcherism has not wiped out the advances made in Scottish theatre in the 1970s. Indeed, as Alasdair Cameron says in *Scotfree*, "Scottish theatre is much more resilient and the various Scottish funding bodies much more enlightened than ... pessimism might have led one to expect." Cameron's selection, four full-length pieces and three shorter ones, is designed to show the range of writing talent currently at work in Scotland. Represented are John Byrne - though *Writer's Cramp*, which launched Byrne's career as a dramatist in 1977, is not 'recent' - John Clifford, Chris Hannan and Tony Roper, the authors of *Losing Venice*, *Elizabeth Gordon Quinn* and *The Steamie*. Alongside these Cameron offers us pieces by Ann Marie di Mambro, Rona Munro and John McKay.

How good to see these plays in print, for one curse of Scottish theatre has been the unavailability in print of even highly successful plays, let alone moderately successful ones. A play is a more fragile creation than a novel or a volume of verse: it is only truly alive in performance, and unless it is revived, re-performed and reinterpreted then its chances of survival are slim. Publication is no substitute for performance but it does ensure that the text is around to be read and talked about, and that can be a stimulus to further performance. The history of play publishing in Scotland is not a cheering one, littered with brave but aborted ventures. One hopes this initiative taken by Nick Hern Books is financially successful.

In his introduction Cameron worries about what constitutes a Scottish play and identifies the "shackles of London" as the inhibiting factor for all non-English, English-speaking theatres. The Canadians, he argues, have managed to draw on French tradition, to create a theatre much more visual than the Anglo-Saxon one, but the Scots have yet to develop their own distinctive style. However he identifies 'serio-comic naturalism' as an important feature of much Scottish writing, a style which owes much to the traditions of the music hall and variety theatre, with their sketches and stand-up comics. Certainly in Byrne's work that influence is clear: the comic invention is extraordinarily fertile, and the one-liners memorable and acute, but the narrative is less sure-footed. Cameron argues that sentimentality remains important in Scottish writing, and is uneasy about its effects, (though reluctant to be too critical, for one piece in his anthology, Tony Roper's The Steamie, touching and amusing as it is, is awash with urban kailyard sentimentality). Above all, says Cameron, Scottish dramatists and their audiences have a shared consciousness which is less class-based and more national than its equivalent south of the border. That in its turn can be related to the lack of a Scottish "Oxbridge", the less important role of private education, and the more left-inclined nature of our politics.

One problem with the Scottish theatre audience is that it tends to share common assumptions rather too cosily. It has been too easy to secure cheap laughs at the expense of the Thatcher government and wax indignant about its iniquities with the certainty of enthusiastic agreement. What has been lacking is a consistent examination of the problems the country faces and the hard choices which will have to be made. The Ship, for example, was a marvellous technical achievement, and much of the action convincing and touching, but did it really help us to understand how we squandered our inheritance as a major shipbuilding nations of the world?

It would be wrong to suggest that the plays in Scotfree are tarred with that uncritical brush. Chris Hannan's Elizabeth Gordon Quinn offers us a heroine who refuses to fit into the working class stereotype, and Rona Munro's Saturday at the Commodore and Ann Marie di Mambro's The Letter Box deal with lesbianism and domestic violence in contemporary Scotland. John Clifford in Losing Venice embarks on a skilful exploration of history, the resonances of which are universal, and have little to do with the traditional concerns of Scottish dramatic writing.

One unhealthy aspect of the Scottish situation is that only some of our theatres are committed to the presentation of new work and the nurturing of indigenous talent. Two full-length plays and one shorter one were presented by the Traverse, one full-length play by Wildcat, the fourth independently and the remaining two short pieces as part of an anthology of new work by 7:84. Three cheers for the Traverse, and other theatres, including the Tron in Glasgow which has recently become more oriented to new writing, but what about the Lyceum, Perth, Pitlochry, Dundee?

Are their records all they ought to be? Cameron praises developments in Canadian dramatic writing; the Canada Council for a number of years has sought to make the presentation of indigenous work a condition of grant. Perhaps the Scottish Arts Council could send someone across the Atlantic on a fact-finding mission.

7:84 Theatre Company (Scotland) has been one of Scotland's liveliest touring companies. Under John McGrath's directorship it built up a repertoire of left-wing plays, mostly by McGrath himself and engaged directly with the concerns of the time. Also 7:84 revived scripts from earlier this century, to demonstrate that there is a tradition of urban naturalism which predates the explosion of such work since the seventies. The recent history of 7:84 has been difficult: after a dispute with the Scottish Arts Council over its artistic direction, McGrath left, to be succeeded by David Hayman, who has continued the 'committed' (ie left-wing) stance of the company but has opened it up to a number of established and new writers. That the events leading up to this 'dropping of the pilot' were unpleasant is clear from McGrath's The Bone Won't Break and his wife's The Moon Belongs to Everyone. McGrath's book consists of lectures he gave at Cambridge Unversity in 1988, in which he discusses the demise of 7:84 (England) and the crisis of leadership at 7:84 (Scotland). McGrath is a bitter man, and does not hesitate to point fingers and name names. It is easy to understand his feelings, but the reader must wonder at the wisdom of venting these feelings so soon after the events which produced them. McGrath demeans himself by some of the things he says here, which would have been better left unsaid. What is valuable is a stimulating discussion of the difficulties which lie in the way of creating a genuine popular culture.

Elizabeth MacLennan's book is basically an autobiography centred, naturally enough, on her work with her husband. It is an impressive story of hard graft under difficult conditions, and while the reader has on occasion to smile at the unending round of protests and demonstrations which had to be fitted into a punishing domestic and theatrical schedule, such energy and commitment can only be admired. MacLennan has plenty to say how her husband was forced to leave 7:84 (Scotland), but her tone is more hurt than bitter. The Moon Belongs to Everyone will no doubt be compulsory reading for the committed enthusiasts 7:84 attracted in its heyday, but even for theatregoers who had their doubts about the effects of the company's ideological orientation, it should prove a fascinating - and at times touching - read.

David Hutchison

AN EXPERIMENT IN LIFE & WORK

Jill Benton, *Naomi Mitchison: A Century of Experiment in Life and Letters*, Pandora Press, 192pp, £15.95; Naomi Mitchison, *A Girl Must Live*, Richard Drew Publishing, 253pp, £12.95.

This timely book repeats material covered in Mitchison's autobiographical works, especially on the childhood years. But it presents the information in a more thorough, chronologically ordered manner and fills in many gaps that Mitchison left tantalisingly open. For example, Mitchison discusses in *You May Well Ask* (1979) the decision taken by herself and her husband, Dick, to have an open marriage and mentions 'lovers' but no names. Benton provides names not only of some of Naomi's lovers, but of Dick's too. She also charts Mitchison's reactions to her husband's lovers, in some cases close friends of hers.

Needless scandalmongering? Well, no. Mitchison was profoundly influenced by people like H T Wade Gery, a classical scholar who encouraged her early "Hellenic period", and with whom she had a longstanding intimate relationship. As a writer Mitchison felt she needed the freedom to know and explore the minds of others with the intimacy that a sexual relationship quickly allows. This kind of thinking was a very important part of the socialist and feminist ideals that she and Dick shared: ideals which prompted them to relinquish ownership of each others' bodies while maintaining a very close and loving relationship. Mitchison actually encouraged and helped Dick in his affairs. Benton points out that although this kind of behaviour was deemed shocking by many it was not unique in its time as many of the couples the Mitchisons were friendly with were experimenting in the same manner.

Benton tirelessly interviewed Mitchison and her family. She has perused documents in libraries or still in Mitchison's possession. The latter include old letters from lovers and friends and even letters between herself and her husband. The contents of such letters are the source of most of the new material in this biography.

Benton states that this is not a book read or approved by Mitchison before publication. Benton undoubtedly has a special relationship with her subject. She has also clearly trodden on dangerous ground with a lady not always receptive to people who wish to lay bare details of her past. In an interview with myself in April 1990 Mitchison said, quite unprompted, of Jill Benton: 'She wanted to skin me alive' - a hint to myself that she did not want to be pushed too hard.

Benton has not allowed her pursuit of the truth to be deflected by Mitchison's reticence on certain subjects: past lovers being one of them.

As she draws towards the end of a long and unusual life, always receptive to new ideas and ready to experiment, she worries that aspects of her past will cause pain and embarrassment to her children and grandchildren. There is also her general maxim that one does not kiss and tell.

Jill Benton's studies on Mitchison began with the PhD thesis she completed in 1986 for the University of California, *Historical Representation in the Novels of Naomi Mitchison (1931-1935)*, about Mitchison as a feminist. This brings a bias to the biography: it is largely a feminist interpretation of Mitchison's life and work. This is a rather narrow interpretation. While Mitchison is concerned with the role of women in society she is interested in much more besides. She herself, as Benton admits, denies the feminist appellation.

Benton describes her first novels, *The Conquered* (1923) and *Cloud Cuckoo Land* (1925), as if they were feminist works with female protagonists: they are really adventure stories with male protagonists, Beric and Alxenor. These books show deep interest in ancient Celtic, Roman and Hellenic culture as well as contemporary political problems: to discuss them as simply feminist tracts both diminishes and distorts the real force behind them. Although her claims for her subject as a ground-breaking feminist may be exaggerated, Benton accurately, on the whole, draws the connections between Mitchison's life and work. This is important for a writer such as Mitchison where life and work are so intimately interwined.

Benton deserves severe criticism for such errors as when she mentions that Mitchison was invited to stand for 'the Dundee seat in Aberdeen' or for misspelling Elizabeth Harman as *Harmon* throughout. But she has got the thing right when she says of Mitchison and her life in Africa:

Naomi lived an unresolvable contradiction, apparent here in the desert as surely as in Carradale and, for that matter, in working-class Birmingham. With the best of intentions Naomi yearned to be part of folk communities, sharing her resources. In Mochudi she had the wherewithal to feed dying babies with her gifts. Naomi's largesse paradoxically placed her above the folk from whom she sought acceptance. Her economic and social class - whether she liked it or not, she was Lady Mitchison - did not square with her socialism. And really, short of giving away most of what she owned, there was little Naomi could do to change this basic contradiction in her life, as painful as it was - and is. (p153)

Considering the problems (not least having a subject not only alive, but kicking) Benton generally strikes a good balance with this controversial and elusive figure. This book is an easier way into Mitchison than the autobiographical material which, being patchy and lacking chronological order, often fails to bring together the strands of personal and emotional experiences with writing and other aspects of outward life. Naomi Mitchison has now found a secure place on the literary map. Her life and work are of interest not only to students of Scottish literature and feminist critics but an indispensable source of information for historians and critics of the socio-political and scientific currents of the Thirties.

Extensive personal contact with Africans, West Scottish folk and others has given Mitchison much of her raw material. She is fond of writing in the first person or from a fixed viewpoint and many stories depend on a narrator whose experience the author, as an upper-class white (albeit more travelled than most), knows only secondhand. The occasional intrusion of upper-class syntax as well as the obvious planting of 'the moral of the tale' in stories like 'A Girl Must Live' or 'Out of the West' do nothing to allay misgivings about the truth of experience portrayed.

Despite (or perhaps because of) her highly-developed social awareness, Mitchison skirts around the inner life of 'low-life' characters with the dogged determination of a Jeffrey Archer. She can also be unforgivably patronising. Laureen, the prostitute turned rich man's wife in 'A Girl Must Live', with her shelf of romantic novels, is not even pathetic - just silly and shallow. That she later finds refuge in a poor African home, complete with sleeping child, seems nothing but a contrived lesson for a wooden character.

Mitchison is at her best when writing Fantasy: when the conventions of realism and experience become indistinct or irrelevant and the most potent force is a vivid and unconventional imagination. Mitchison may make an unconvincing oppressed black person, but she can be a pretty convincing dragon. There are delicate comic undertones in "Nagli's First Princess", an account of a young dragon who botches his first treasure-collecting assignment. In this story Mitchison incorporates, in light-hearted manner, favourite themes such as the generation gap, differences which block understanding, and the fact that most beautiful things neither last forever nor are easy to acquire. Those who have read *Travel Light* will be familiar with her sympathetic portayal of the comically acquisitive dragons.

"Miss Omega Raven" is more serious, but the story of the raven's troubles and success is moving and thought-provoking. Told from the raven's perspective and bound by her limited knowledge, the tale is necessarily and effectively simple, an unusual mix of science fiction and animal fable with the shadowy idea of a mind-tinkering scientist etched in the bird's consciousness. This scientist has given the raven the mixed blessing of heightened awareness, which nearly causes her complete and irreversible downfall but in the end allows her to break the stagnant conventions of status in raven society and achieve the highest accolade: the 'top raven' as her mate.

Mitchison's distaste for conventions and rules is reflected in that of the raven's. Disregarding the rules leads Mitchison sometimes to create refreshingly original stories like 'Miss Omega Raven'. Equally often this disregard leads her to write stories and poems which are less than satisfactory. Both are represented in *A Girl Must Live*, the title itself a plea for canny judgment.

Joyce M Salazar

SCOTCH MIST PENETRATED

Peter Womak, *Improvement and Romance: Constructing the Myth of the Highlands*, MacMillan.

Historians should not, ashen faced at the prospect of francophile theory penetrating north of Fort William, close this book on discovering that Dr Womak's model for perceiving the post-1745 Highlands is derived from Roland Barthes' definition of mythology, an area colonised "by an empire of signs". Though theoretical jargon does, on occasion, clot Womak's prose, this is balanced by the book's provocative, acerbic intelligence and its erudition in a mass of writing about the Highlands which he has resurrected. Who among us has heard of John O'Keeffe's Boswell's tour-derived *The Highland Reel?*

The book is also a major contribution to the vexed problem of using literary texts as historical evidence. In principle, Womak, commits the crime common to the new historicism that sees all literary texts as (in Robert Alter's words) "a reflection in any society of the values of the ruling class, abetted by a learned or priestly elite". Younger academics often have a power-derived fantasy that the fate of empires depends on how literary departments treat the texts they choose to teach. To quote Alter again, "the literary imagination develops a momentum of its own, in indifference or in actual contravention to reigning ideology". What saves Womak is that he is dealing not with works of imagination but ephemeral literary fantasies, products of the dominant ideology of their age. The Highlands attracted fanciful writers like midges. Womak, therefore, rarely has the problem of dealing, as occasionally in Burns, with a genuinely imaginative response to the land and its people. Oddly, too, in someone who so stresses the repression of the Highland voice, Womak has little to say of past or present

Highland creative writing. Gunn, Sorley MacLean and Crichton Smith would have added tangibly to his cause. However, Womak's interpretations are directly descended from the modified Marxism of Raymond Williams's *The Country and the City*, with its penetrating scepticism concerning bourgeois pastoralism's troubled, often illusory, relationship with the world it had left behind.

In chapters devoted to militarism, terrain, the supernatural and social organisation, Womak traces the relationships of two apparently contradictory phenomena which appeared after the 1745, the Adam Smith-derived ideology of Improvement and the flood of sentimental writing about the Highlands. Their contradiction is that while one stresses the economic practicality of development, the other enthusiastically broods over a landscape of emptiness and loss. Womak is least convincing when he tries to display a direct connection between these phenomena. His argument that bourgeois progress needed a falsely edenic world of compensatory fantasy to set against the anxieties of its own chosen, economically individualistic historical path is more cogent and revealing. Womak believes that the intensity of this Highland fantasy created in non-Highland minds a "reality", a Highland "otherness", which set the Highlanders paralysingly apart, contributing to their economic decay.

The book is informative on examples of the Highlanders as plastic projections of Lowland Scottish and subsequent British political, economic and psychological compulsions. Womak is particularly convincing and incisive on the Pitt-inspired metamorphosis of the Highlanders from bestial insurrectionaries to ultra-loyal "indispensable atavistic natives in the Victorian triumph of peace and progress". He is also excellent on "Ossian" MacPherson's employment of eighteenth-century aesthetics to fill empty space with bad poetry and to satisfy the ambiguous erotically morbid craving for the supernatural or an increasingly secular age. He also argues convincingly against seeing Ossian as a national epic and relates wittily its "suppression of the genital with a historical nation which doesn't reproduce itself."

Though as a Marxist Womak is uneasy with nationalism, the book is also revealing about the sorry story of the evolution of Scottish nationalism in terms of fake Celticism. The Lowland Scots hated the Highlanders. An early Lowland mediaeval poem contemplates God's creation of the slothful, thieving Highlander from a horse turd. Later, the satire in Defoe and Fielding regarding the political consequences of Jacobite militarism came from genuine terror. Womak has a weakness for seeing the oppressed as victims. During Bute's term of office, the Lowland Scots in England were tarred with the Highland brush. This insult the Lowlanders shook off and, inspired by Scott, created a national identity committed to the imperial British state and emotionally attached to a Scotland largely compounded of narcissistic "Highland" fantasy: "for the Scottish bourgeoisie, therefore, the Highlands had the aspect of residual historical nation - a reminder of an economic stagnation they were relieved to have left behind, but also an accreditation of the national identity which was both required and eroded by their participation in the imperial adventure." It is still uncertain how this toxic fantasy operates in the Scottish bloodstream.

Andrew Noble

AN ORDINARY WOMAN?

Mary & Hector MacIver, *Pilgrim Souls*, Aberdeen University Press

"This is the story of a man who was extraordinary and a woman who was ordinary, who came from two very different backgrounds." Given the nature of this biography/autobiography, where Mary writes three sections and 'edits' an assortment of Hector's writings, it is the personality of the 'ordinary' Mary MacIver that emerges most vividly, and in all its human complexity. Indeed, it could hardly be otherwise, in these circumstances. I suspect, also, that in this book as in life, Mary disregarded Ben Jonson's focus on the demonstrative adjective in his qualified admiration for Shakespeare: "I loved the man, and do honour his memory, on *this* side idolatry." When a woman finds "one man (who) loved the pilgrim soul" of her, it is expecting too much to look for balanced response, especially when premature parting leads her to/ Murmur, a little sadly, how love fled/ And paced upon the mountains overhead/ And hid his face amid a crowd of stars."

This book shows that the term 'ordinary woman' is meaningless. Hector's extraordinariness, however, is defined too exclusively in terms of his Celtic roots and identity. "People like Hugh MacDiarmid, Louis MacNeice and Dylan Thomas all saw in Hector not just a fascinating personality in his own right, and a wonderful raconteur, but also the representative of a world that they would either have liked to grow up in... or to have had much more personal contact with." I'd have liked more on "in his own right".

The first part concerns Mary's upbringing in the mining village of Gorebridge till, via University, she went to teach in Portobello High School. Having followed a similar pattern in a nearby mining community, I can vouch for the accuracy of detail - moleskin trousers, carbide lamps, galvanised tin baths, semmits, rag-rugs, Knox the Butcher, MacNab the Chemist, Soor Plooms and Ogopogo Eyes, the Gothenburg, the Picture House. And yet, something is missing - maybe the neighbourliness, the sense of community. There is a detached quality in Mary's recollections that applies to more than the WRI. "We were not participants, merely onlookers, for not only would my father not join anything but he would never allow us to do so either." It is an accurate picture, but one of living in a community without ever being part of it.

The second part, inevitably since a composite of Hector's writings (scripts for broadcast, informal letters, autobiographical notes, lectures) is jerky and uneven, but offers a helpful chronology that takes us from his upbringing in Shawbost on Lewis, via the Nicholson Institute, Edinburgh University and the Royal Navy, to Portobello High School. An entry in Marian McNeill's 'The Silver Bough' sets the tone. There are responses to the mystery of the cycle of the seasons, Hogmanay, 'the Night of Cakes', the Atlantic, second sight, Kirk and Ceilidh cheek by jowl with the impact of the sinking of the Iolaire, the Spanish 'flu, and highly personal literary comments on Johnson, Boswell and Ossian. Hector's threads of white, scarlet and black are interwoven through this section, to the everpresent music of *puirt-a-beul* and waulking song.

I enjoyed a privileged apprenticeship under Hector MacIver at the Royal High School; he was the most inspiring teacher of Romantic poetry and drama I have met. This was a different Hector, though the roots of the teacher and his enthusiasms are clearly discernible.

The final two parts are a poignant narration of the relationship of Hector and Mary, his premature death, her sense of isolation, her finding a sanctuary in painting. It is, basically, a love story, sad, frank, tender - yet oddly interspersed with dismissive comment of anonymous teaching colleagues, Moray House, even members of the MacIver family that jar slightly. Conversely, Mary's determination "to keep his memory green, and to make people see what an unforgettable human being he was" has rested too much on identifying the 'names' of Hector's world - MacDiarmid, Goodsir Smith, MacCaig, Dylan Thomas, Sorley MacLean, MacNiece, Sir William Gillies, Grierson, Wolfit, Causley and runs the danger of creating of a coterie. 'Ordinary' women don't overcome a profound shyness to write their autobiography or have exhibitions of their paintings. The real impact of *Pilgrim Souls* is how love of an extraordinary man has effected this transformation.

Sandy Forsyth

Theatre Roundup

Glasgow was the European City of Culture in 1990, and all attempts to pretend that it didn't happen are idle. This year, the western metropolis has been spared the embarrassment of trying to fit prestigeful foreign productions into unsuitable venues, but one result was that Mayfest felt more than usually ragged around the edges.

Of the better offerings, much would have been done anyway. At the Tron, Michael Boyd gave a strong, intelligent production of another play by the French-Canadian Michel Tremblay, *The Real Wurld?*, a translation into Scots, apparently nearer in spirit to the original than is English. I fear I never really felt much bothered about the main protagonist Claude, who takes a sabbatical from middle-class Montreal to scribble down recollections about his childhood, comprising a welter of dark family secrets which may include incest. Many theatre-goers found this a fine, moving play; and there is no doubting its seriousness of intent, nor that it was splendidly performed.

The rejuvenated 7:84 company celebrated its new start with what might be called a political farce, *Revolting Peasants*. This has been the first 7:84 production for a long time offering anything that might be classed as actual entertainment - and entertainment, moreover, with the sort of popular appeal for which the company has striven; during its tour, parties of people drove quite a long way to see it a second time.

But there are depressing caveats. Apart from the dreary superficiality of the humour itself (though all credit to the cast), the wretched poll tax is surely a clapped-out target. I remember three or four years ago seeing a visiting one-man show, *Poll-Axed*, which dealt with the same topic far more wittily, intelligently and succinctly when it was more of a burning issue. Are there not more fertile fields to be furrowed? Could no-one do something about the Adam Smith Institute, whose desperately-intense spokesmen seem so often only a step away from wild self-parody?

Amongst other questions raised by shows like *Revolting Peasants* is the continuing one of whether 'popular' Scottish theatre is achievable or even possible. But leaving that well-worked seam alone, allow me tentatively to pose a different problem. Are there any of our writers prepared to come out with *positive* vision? It is true that the poll tax and other baneful aspects of present-day Britain (or the world) are fit targets for attack, satirical or otherwise; that criticism might be easy does not imply its being either unnecessary or invalid. But instead of concentrating on things that should be done away with, is nobody prepared to come forward with an idea of what a better world would look like, and what sort of lives the people therein might live?

I am not looking for glib answers along the lines of 'property-owning democracy', or 'full-blooded socialism'. What I am hoping for would be a description of the environment in which (say) the no-hopers who figure so largely in the work of James Kelman would find fulfillment and happiness? Too difficult an undertaking? There have been a surprising number of exercises in practical utopianism since Sir Thomas More (or, perhaps, Plato) first defined the genre. They include William Morris's News From Nowhere and Aldous Huxley's Island, both lovely though unconvincing volumes. There has also been Bridie's Holy Isle, put on at the Edinburgh Festival several years ago and much jeered at. Yet it is surely one of Bridie's best plays, for all that it was little fitted to the taste of the drab, sneering 'eighties.

The disappointment of Mayfest was Chris Hannan's The Evil Doers, justified since great things are regularly expected of Chris Hannan, and an incisive expose of that seedy slab of Glasgow's life which continues unaffected by city-centre stone-cleaning, civic publicity campaigns, new shopping precincts and cultural awards promised appetising fare. Not one of Hannan's best, but even so deserving better than the flaccid, uneven production it was accorded here.

One of Mayfest's best successes was an import from Edinburgh's Traverse, Bondagers by Sue Glover, who is bidding fair to become the Nigel Tranter of the Scottish stage. She wrote one play, set in a highland croft, about a seal-woman who turned out to be a dangerously slippery customer; and another play, set in a northern island, based on the sad tale of Lady Grange. Bondagers was better than either of these. A fuller appreciation, by a different hand, concludes this article.

From the ashes of the intermittently-active but sometimes excellent Theatre Co-Op there has arisen - in phoenix-like fashion - the new company Fifth Estate which has the advantage of a smidgeon of official funding, and will present a new George Rosie play at the Fringe; meanwhile, I and all too few others are immensely grateful to them for Bernard de Como's We, Charles XII, the best new play I've come across for some time.

The work is a powerful exemplar of how history can be used to explore and illumine the mores of an unmistakably contemporary age. The Charles of the title is the Swedish monarch (1697-1718) who had from early youth an insatiable relish for soldiering, and fortunately some talent for it as well. He carried out a number of enormous campaigns, which took him and his hard-driven troops over vast tracts of Europe.

De Como's central character is a man obsessed with his next victory, of ego so inflated there is no corner for consideration of his army's welfare, far less the love of women. His obsession is first amusing, then intriguing, finally maddening; it survives unweakened through disaster and even the humiliation of beggarly supplicancy at the court of the Grand Turk. Charles is the dominating fulcrum of the action, but the play is well-populated around the periphery, allowing for generous infusions of wit and compassion.

It is too simple to describe this as a long metaphor for avarice and cupidity, for this human play affords more subtlety and satisfaction than so trite a description can suggest. Fifth Estate's production was scarcely lavish, but amply adequate to its purposes and often excellent; Sandy Neilson's performance as Charles's spivvish court sycophant was magnificent.

Lastly, another disappointment: Radio 4's Kaleidoscope recently had a programme dealing with reviewers, and how actors felt about bad notices. Alert for phrases to plagiarise, I listened attentively. The actors gave the best value, some going to inordinate lengths to declare their lack of resentment; but there were few really sharp critical barbs on offer. Diana Rigg did however disclose that once, playing a nude scene, she had been described as "a mausoleum insufficiently supplied with flying butresses". Ungallant, that.

Alasdair Simpson

Note: Those who went to Bondagers by Sue Glover fearing a swing merely from the urban kailyard back to the rural were pleasantly surprised to find a strong, tautly written portrayal of a female underclass of virtual slaves who kept the Lothian and Borders farms going throughout the previous century. Glover had done her homework on this phenomenon, briefly that men were feed, or arled, to farms not only on the strength of their own skill and experience, but on that of their women too, who put their energies to whatever tasks were seasonally necessary. The strong Traverse cast made this a whirling, beautifully-moved production which was quite spellbinding.

One potential strength was the natural, East-coast Scots which the play attempted, but here was an opportunity missed, for the Scots was inconsistently spoken with some wierd and wonderful cadences never before heard on any hill or howe - not the fault of the actors but more a comment on the neglect of Scots in drama schools. This can be put right in a new production, if Glover works on the language, and a coach is employed who knows Border Scots. After all, the language is still vigorously spoken only a few miles from Edinburgh's Traverse Theatre. Otherwise a triumph for native Scots drama. - JH.

Pamphleteer

Thomas Land's *Free Women* (The National Poetry Foundation, 27 Mill Road, Fareham, Hants, £4) is "an essay about loneliness in the sex war." And yet, this supposition seems lacking in substance considering the content of the poems themselves. Land clearly acknowledges the inequalities between the sexes, yet fails to offer any new insights into how this alienates sex from sex or gives voice to the differing experiences of gender-associated loneliness. Typical is the voice of Margot the whore who tells of men who "whipped me hard/ and dragged me by the breasts, but when the gracious/ stern tyrant turned his mood and chose to charm/ me into bed, I flew with desire whatever/ my woes." There is no understanding here: only a rehashing of stereotypes that regrettably crop up throughout the collection as men "exploitative, cunning, suspicious and mean" and women who feed themselves "to the piercing milkteeth/ of family." Land expresses eloquent sympathy for the subjugation of women, but in a tone that lends itself to superciliousness and lack of originality.

He writes better in *Berlin Proposal* (Envoi Poets Publications, Pen Fford, Newport, Dyfed, £3) where the poems stand authentic and strong in condemnation of indifference and death of passion. In 'I Sing You A Song', Land catches perfectly the sense of the world dying around us with our hands seemingly tied behind our backs: "I sing of the nectar of fluttering butterflies/ of our doubtful obsolete balance of terror/ of the omen of routed dying birds/ limping across the sky". Land's concern with "green issues" is spiced here with the wisdom of insight and careful imagery that makes this worthy and readable.

Tom Leonard in *nora's place* (Galloping Dog Press, £3.50) invites us to step into the small mundane world that nora inhabits, populated more by the endless tins of "dog food/ birds eye codsteaks/ hamburgers" on supermarket shelves than by friends and family. The ordinary comes under the microscope here: worries are about who will walk the dog and whether to give the children chips twice a day. Leonard allows us to step into a life oppressed by normality and banality. A sense of need and loss rings throughout the poems, his gift being to draw out the simple truths that unspoken add to the emptiness of unfulfilled lives: "I wish you would touch me more/ it makes me feel happy/ and secure".

In *The New Hesperides* by David Gill and Sally Cottis (95 Harefields, Oxford, £1.50) there is no lack of touching. For this pseudo-erotica is dedicated to Robert Herrick, now centuries dead, who spent his time creating a "rich assortment of love-poems." Gill's tribute to Herrick comes as a batch of love-poems written in a "modern vein". It is impossible to estimate Herrick's reaction to this, but bemusement might well be critically appropriate. For example, Gill becomes rhapsodic at the sight of a beauty "talcing like one demented/ your armpits and your breasts" and is almost beside himself in 'Onion Girl': "Deeper still the layers go:/ the faint lines of your bra/ suggest another truth below./ That's where your nipples are." Harmless enough, these make an interesting diversion, if not great literary impact.

Nothing as light-hearted, however, is to be found in *Out From Beneath The Boot* by Bobby Christie (Neruda Press, 51 Allison Street, Crosshill, £1). Here poetry is used as a political motivator: "Poetry/ could be an/ act of violence/ against the/ state." In minimalist stanza, Christie's poems are direct and forceful: the words hit you like punches. Christie does not care for the sensitivities of his readers, for his concerns are the real misery and sufferings of the people - be they living and dying in Nicaragua or in a Glasgow scheme. Brutally succinct, each poem drives its message home, matching the violence of the streets with Christie's violent convictions for a world without poverty or injustice.

To Travel Hopefully by Alistair Halden (Envoi Publications, Pen Fford, Newport, Dyfed, £2) is more gentle. Full of stark, natural imagery Halden writes in calm and subtle tones. His words trace the progress of the wings of gulls as they glide through the sky and give colour and substance to giant cliffs that grace the seashore. Halden's concern is the natural world and man's need to belong to it. In "Letter of Resignation - 22nd June" he states his reasons for leaving the firm:

Mine is no sworn denial before cockcrow,
No clandestine exchange of silver pieces,
Simply a wish to tramp the heather hills,
And contemplate the world's variety.

The simplicity here allows the sincerity of Halden's feelings to shine through - shaping and defining the collection from within.

Writing in a competent and graceful style, Eddie McGrory in *Illuminations - An Eighth Collection* wanders over pastoral territories. His writing is often imbued with a sense of religious mysticism as he muses gently over the wonders of birdsong and the blossoming wayside flower. Yet greater than this is a sense of nostalgia and the realisation of not only the "Ephemerality of love" but of life also. "Old lions", "ghostly larks" and "the eighty year cold finger/ bare/ Of wedding ring" are symbols of recurring themes that emerge through McGrory's work and which lend themselves to the *requiescat* feel of the collection.

Appearing in three volumes are Keith Harris's *Maid Of The Mystic Now* poems: *Cupid's Anon, Colours in chiarascuro* and *Tomorrow's Troubling Today*. Intriguing titles, but not so enticing is the barrage of information that lurks between the covers. We are told that the trilogy is dedicated to Our Lady of the Mystic Present and that the poems are an attempt "to catch that moment of meeting love at first sight." However, these words are deceptively simple, for as we begin Cupid's Anon - the complex assault on our minds unfolds.

Pregnant with mysticism, his poems display a verbal dexterity and range that is impressive but inaccessible. 'Poem 2' tells us there is a place beyond our definition of boundaries where "the soar of the Archer's Bow,/ untroubled by starches boding in gravity,/ resonates trackless/ beyond mountains and the weal of nations/ and a logic/ grating extrapolated yesterdays/ to scabs". Similar "anarchic heathendom struggles" flourish into the next two volumes. This creates an overbearing intensity that causes the mind to cloud over, lost in the confusion of high metaphor, distant philosophy and rare words. Harris also adds his own criticism, invites us to note his "haiku-like imagery" and "assonances and illiterations playing upon rhythms." Backed up by eccentric footnotes - "How fascinating that the modern English night and knight are pronounced identically" - not a book to retain your sanity by.

Mystical too, is *Flight Into Reality* by Rosemary Rowley (Rowan Tree Press, An Clophreas, Caorthainn). But its roots remain firmly in the ground with the right balance of heaven-bound thoughts and cruel realities of city living. In 20 cantos, fronted by a quote from Dante, Shakespeare or the Bible, Rowley's poetry is based upon the Egyptian legend of Isis and Osiris. With individual flair, Rowley shows through a modern-day search for love the erosion of the soul which has caused "an inner lack of wholeness" to become "the hall-mark of our civilisation". Rowley is best in Canto 2 where her outpourings of grief at her loved one's death are magnificent. Using the universe as her soapbox, Rowley expresses the rage found in grief and a sense of personal and worldly loss as powerful as the laments of Cleopatra at the death of Anthony.

If this power is not maintained throughout, then the range and originality of imagery is. Rowley's vision incorporates the actions of angels where they grab "Back the curtains of the world on Mondays/ Wishing to be human, wishing to blab/ And touch, after the ecstatic Sundays/ To go AWOL and experience skin". This ambitious project works; held together by its freshness and insight - refreshing and stimulating poetry.

Sara Evans

Catalogue

The cataloguist's eyes light up: Walter Bower reappears: Volume 5 of *Scotichronicon* in the Aberdeen University Press (£35.00), Latin and translation - a treasurehouse of Scottish history. (£35) Alexander II, III, Thomas the Rymer, the Rymer, the 1224 strike at Inchcolm Priory! The Albigensian crusade! Omit nothing! One likewise looks forward to more of the Duke-Edinburgh edition of *The Letters of Jane Welsh & Thomas Carlyle* (£35.65 per vol). But did the Carlyles really have a showerbath fitted in 1843, one which disappointed a certain guest? But none of the huge scholarship devoted to the project has yet ascertained *how* the showerbath disappointed! Shame! Fie! Etc! Jestings aside, an appeal continues to raise funds for this huge venture, c/o Old College, South Bridge, Edinburgh EH1.

Grant F. Wilson's *A Bibliography of Iain Crichton Smith* (AUP £8.95) is thorough, and well-produced. It could have been easier to use *and* even cheaper. ICS seems not to need Peter Finch's *How to Publish Your Poetry* "a practical guide/ completely revised and updated". (Alison & Busby, £6.99). Horace advised "Put your parchment in the closet & keep it back till the ninth year", cf. *Envoi Book of Quotes on Poetry*, C. Hammond (Envoi £3).

Outstanding is *Don't Look Back, Jack!* (Canongate £12.95) traveller tales from Duncan Williamson, extraordinary traditional tale-teller of vast repertoire, about the legendary figure 'Jack', in splendid Scots. More modern is *A Roomful of Birds*, Scottish Short Stories 1990 (Collins), authors mostly young & established. *Homeland* (Simon & Schuster, £14.99) is a triple-decker, billed as "E V Thompson writing as James Munro". The easy prose & plot of the bestselling historical novelist contrast with Thomas Hamilton's 1827 *The Youth & Manhood of Cyril Thornton* (AS-LS): prose of a mannered sort Pallisered of late tho drole when read by Alasdair Gray. "A shot struck him in a vital part, & he fell beneath me." There's nice Scots dialogue, but interest is mainly documentary, Tobacco-Lord Glasgow/Peninsular Wars. This edition by Maurice Lindsay has 440 footnotes, good binding, no expense spared.

Stuart Reid's *The Campaigns of Montrose* (Mercat Press) intriguingly is a book about Montrose's military actions, with all the strange poetry of battle, its special psychology, highlighted by a scholarly treatment. *Girls in their Prime* ed. Paterson & Fewell (Scottish Academic Press, £8.50) is a series of essays on women-&-Scottish-education, current social & historical *Forschungen*. One has to be wary where historians too often fabricate cheap victories by pretending to overthrow what they illiterately call 'myths'. Many to whom an exceptional education was available in Victorian Scotland campaigned passionately for open access. In Vol.II of John Donald's *People & Society in Scotland* (ed. Fraser & Morris, £12.50 - the completed work to be reviewed later) Helen Corr offers the comment: "An educational ladder based on open access was fallacy for the bulk of the population growing up in 1914." Not the whole truth, but decrying past Scottish education on the basis of facts all too plain to past educators is a sick sport of current educationalists & historians. Are real abuses not being tied too much into a monolithic schema, with forfeit of perspective?

John Donald's valuable geographical books now include Jim Crumley's *Discovering The Pentland Hills* (£7.50) & John Kerr's *Old Roads in Atholl* (£9.95) both, like many good Scottish journeys, with much to look at, thoroughly informative & not dry. Polygon publish *Voices from the Hunger Marches* "Volume 1" compiled by Ian MacDougall (£9.95). This is a substantial transcription of good material though one hopes the mass of such oral history as gets printed will not foster more cliches and stereotypes. The witnesses are lively and independent.

The real variousness of Scotland is ill-recognised, as the Orcadian Muir saw, & MacDiarmid recognised with cranked-up theories pointing to a need for deep cultural study. One is glad of such as Gordon Donaldson's *A Northern Commonwealth* (Saltire Society, £10.95), going into the ancient Norse past & following right through to present evidences of affinity, showing diversity at an obvious level, kindling useful suspicions. Early Scots Calvinists thought reference to Fortuna, or luck, blasphemy & a sin worse than the games of Dainty Davie, one of many wonders told in *The People's Past*, a wondrous group of essays ed. Edward J. Cowan, (£7.95) one of two very welcome Polygon reissues, beside *Elegies for the Dead in Cyrenaica* (£6.95) by a contributor to the Cowan book, Hamish Henderson, of late also performer in a film *Play me Something* based on a short story by John Berger, cf. Berger's *Once in Europa* (Granta Books, £4.99). More established on the screen, Brian Cox in *Salem to Moscow - An Actor's Odyssey* (Methuen £14.99) reveals a family background in McGonagall's Irish Dundee, & an awakening within the proud culture which survived in the Russian theatre.

Why, a Scottish historian asked this cataloguist, are Scottish-schooled students both surprised by multidisciplinary North American institutions which echo former Scots ones, & incurious, culturally apathetic in drastic contrast with their East European contemporaries? See too Bloodaxe's *Seeds of Fire* ed. Barme & Minford (£7.95), a huge anthology *Chinese Voices of Conscience*, thrown into relief by events in Tianamnen Square: fiction, poetry, documents, even a bit of post-Freud on the Chinese & sex. Real too is Ranginui Walker's *Ka Whawhai Tonu Matou (Struggle Without End)* (Penguin £9.99) gives as a Maori history of New Zealand fresh sight of a country where "half the population are Scots & the other half envious", whose barbarians are its educationists.

Angel Books' list adds now the Austrian Adalbert Stifter (1805-68), *Brigitta* (£6.95), publishing with the title tale the stories 'Abdias', 'Limestone', 'The Forest Path', tr. Helen Watanabe-O'Kelly. Nietzsche expressed admiration for Stifter, for his sober reaction to Romantic style, thoughtful, painstaking. This translation is too conservative of German idiom & at times sentence-structure. Between impressively developed description lame phrases occur, where instead of "was glistening" the river "glistened" unidiomatically. Formality in the English of Adam Zamoyski, translating Henryk Siekiewicz's *Charcoal Sketches* & other tales (Angel £6.95), can work to suprising effect. Freud is translated by the seasoned Manheim/Hull partnership as having noted "I evidently still have a traumatic hyperaesthesia toward dwindling correspondence." (The Freud/-Jung Letters, Penguin £7.99). The words may fit doubts about translations. Douglas Dunn's *Andromache* from Racine (Faber £4.99) was splendidly done by Radio Scotland's drama department last year, and appears in this welcome edition. Dunn's translation is fluent and masterly.

Norman Mailer's *Fight* (Penguin £5.99), about a man to whom Valda Grieve likened her husband, "invades Hemingway territory" says its splurge. Mark Spilka's *Hemingway's Quarrel with Androgyny* (University of Nebraska £37.95) may be worth setting beside that, though unlike Penguin's splurger not calling George Foreman & Muhammad Ali "great minds". *Whatever You Desire* - "A book of lesbian poetry/Edited by Mary Jo Bang", (Oscars Press, BM Oscars, London WC1N 3XX, £4.95) has seriousness/ relevance/ good writing not usually expected in general poetry anthologies. As has *Exchanges* "Poems by Women in Wales" ed. Jude Brigley (Honno Poetry, 'Ailsa Craig', Heol y Cawl, Dinas Powys, De Morgannwg CF6 4AH, £3.95), a good selection of modern Welsh poetry. *Anvil New Poets* ed. Graham Fawcett (Anvil £7.95) interests, with Valerie Thornton, the excellent Indian poet Bibhu Padhi, & more. Desmond O'Grady's version of *The Seven Arab Odes* (Agenda, £6.60), good in parts, strays to overcolloquial or overalliterative like parody Basil Bunting.

Notes on Contributors

J K Annand: associate of MacDiarmid, author of bairnrhymes in mould of
Soutar. Books (*Sing it Aince for Pleisure*) widely used in schools.
Michael Begg: b. Edinburgh 1966, under Gemini. Still here, teaching
creative writing through Artlink and MAMH, and practising same.
Aonghas-Phàdraig Caimbeul: à Uibhist-a-Deas, 's e 'n-dràsda na Sgrìob-
haiche aig Sabhal Mòr Ostaig san Eilean Sgitheanach. Tha a chiad leabhar
bàrdachd aige, *The Greatest Gift*, gu bhith air fhoillseachadh san Dàmh-
air; nobhal Gàidhlig o Acair às a dheaghaidh sin.
James B Caird: born West Linton, Graduated under Sir Herbert Grierson at
Edinburgh University before teaching English and becoming an HMI. His
love of Scots stayed with him from childhood until his death in 1989.
Kate Calder: Principal teacher Guidance & English at Dunfermline High.
Jim Crumley: b. Dundee 1947; 24 years journalist, full-time writer since
1988. Books on Scottish landscape, (*A High and Lonely Place*), 1991.
Matthew Fitt: b. Dundee 1968. Supports Dundee FC; now 'on tour' in
Europe. Watches 'Neighbours' & mentions a dislike for 'Bouncer'.
Paula Fitzpatrick: b. 1951; a mother since 1975, won Brooke-Bond Travel
Scholarship for creative writing in 1969, now writing again.
George Friel (1916-1975): primary-school assist. head, author of novels
(*Mr Alfred MA*) and short stories about life in his native Glasgow.
Innis Macbeath: 5 years a journalist with *Glasgow Herald* then 16 with *The
Times*. Now 62; appeals secretary for Iona Cathedral Trust since 1984.
Alastair Mackie: b. Aberdeen 1925. Former schoolteacher, now a well-
established poet and translator writing in Scots. Lives in Anstruther.
Angus Martin: postman living in Kintyre. His collection, *The Larch Plant-
ation*, recently won SAC Book Award.
John Murray: b. Gold Coast, raised Fife & London. Landscape Architect.
Thom Nairn: Managing editor, *Cencrastus*, writer in residence, Ross &
Cromarty, thesis completed on Sydney Goodsir Smith.
David Purves: b. 1924 Selkirk. Author, *Trace Element Contamination of
the Environment*, Elsevier 1977 (2nd ed 1985); editor, Lallans.
Iain Crichton Smith: distinguished writer in both Gaelic and English;
recently retired from the Literature Committee of the SAC.
Oonagh Warke: b. Castlerock (on the north coast of County Derry), now
an archivist living and working in Dublin.
Jim C Wilson: Stirling District writer in residence, 1989-91; now writing
prose, poems and short stories at his residence in Stockbridge, Edinburgh.

Editorial note: I'd like to correct the unintentional impression given in
Robert Crawford's article that Edwin Morgan did not teach Scottish
literature in the English Literature Department at Glasgow. The department
was progressive in teaching Scot-lit of all periods and Morgan played a
prominent role, continuing to stimulate interest among students even after
the Scottish Department gained its independence. Also Elizabeth Burns'
'Pamphleteer' column is ambiguous about the authorship of the Rimbaud
translation, 'The Sleeper in the Howe', which is in fact by Alastair Mackie.